D N A

WHO'S YOUR DADDY?

D N A

WHO'S YOUR DADDY?

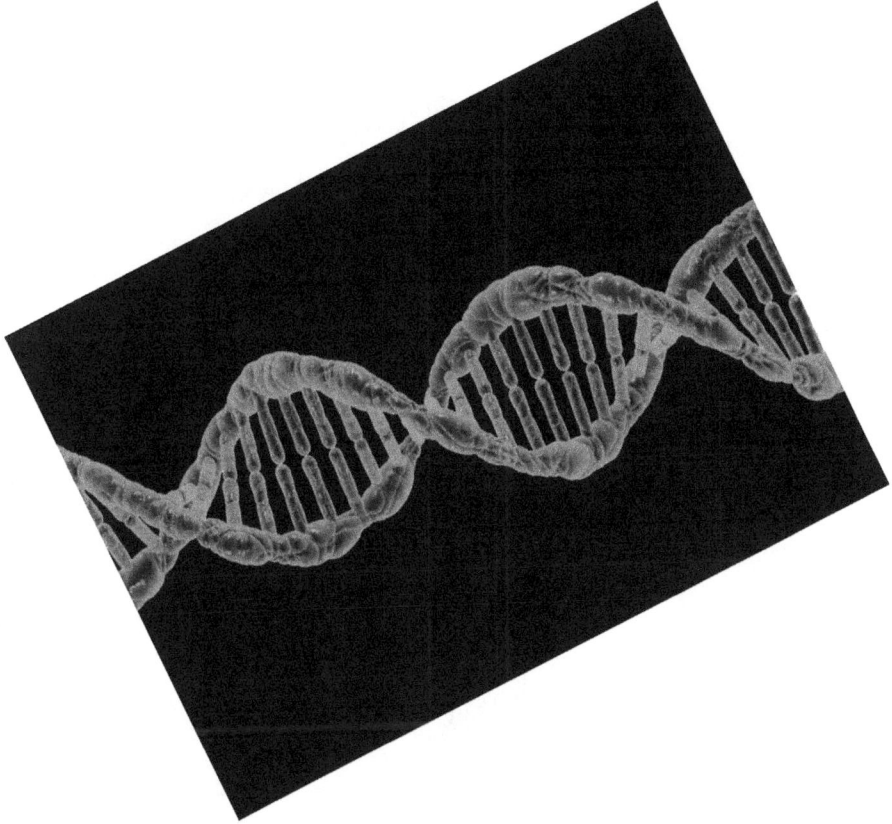

FIDEL M. DONALDSON

Additional Books by the Author

Diamond in the Rough

Don't Birth an Ishmael in the Waiting Room

From the Pit to the Prison to the Palace

It's Time to Come out of Lo-debar

Mercy and the Sufficiency of Grace

Midnight

Perceive and Receive

Praise Worship and the Spirit of Prophecy

The Power of Persistent Prayer

D N A

Who's your Daddy?

"Whereby are given unto us exceeding great and precious promises: that by these ye might be partakers of the divine nature, having escaped the corruption that is in the world through lust" (2 Peter 1:4).

Fidel M. Donaldson

D N A

ISBN: 9780982771068

LCCN: 2015920916

ACKNOWLEDGEMENTS

Dedicated to Abba Father who revealed Himself in fullness through the Lord Jesus Christ, Yeshua Hamashiach! Special thanks to Ingrid Hunter, Sherrie Roberts, Dr. Ronald Ackerson for reading and adding to the richness of this book. To my wife for life, Lady Paulette Donaldson, a.k.a Mrs. Cutie Cutie. I thank the Lord Jesus for you and the joy that I have in the journey because you are by my side.

CONTENTS

INTRODUCTION

ACKNOWLEDGEMENTS

Introduction

In a time when so many people claim a religious affiliation or some connection to God, how do we determine who the true Sons of God are? I believe the way to accomplish that is to do a spiritual DNA test. The spiritual DNA paternity test will determine if the individual has what I call, The *Divine Nature Of Abba*. Religious affiliation and church membership does not make a person a child of God. The children of God have His Divine Nature and that nature is the determining factor in how he or she lives his or her life. Without God's Divine Nature, the religious person can have a form of godliness, but their human nature will manifest, especially when they are tested. Someone once told me, "Only what's inside of a person can come out of them." It sounds very simplistic, but that statement is very profound. The life of a true child of God should exude and exhibit the characteristics and attributes of His Divine Nature. Anyone can claim God as their Father, but when a DNA sample is taken, will the test results come back positive or negative? Who's your Daddy?

Chapter 1

DNA: NATURAL

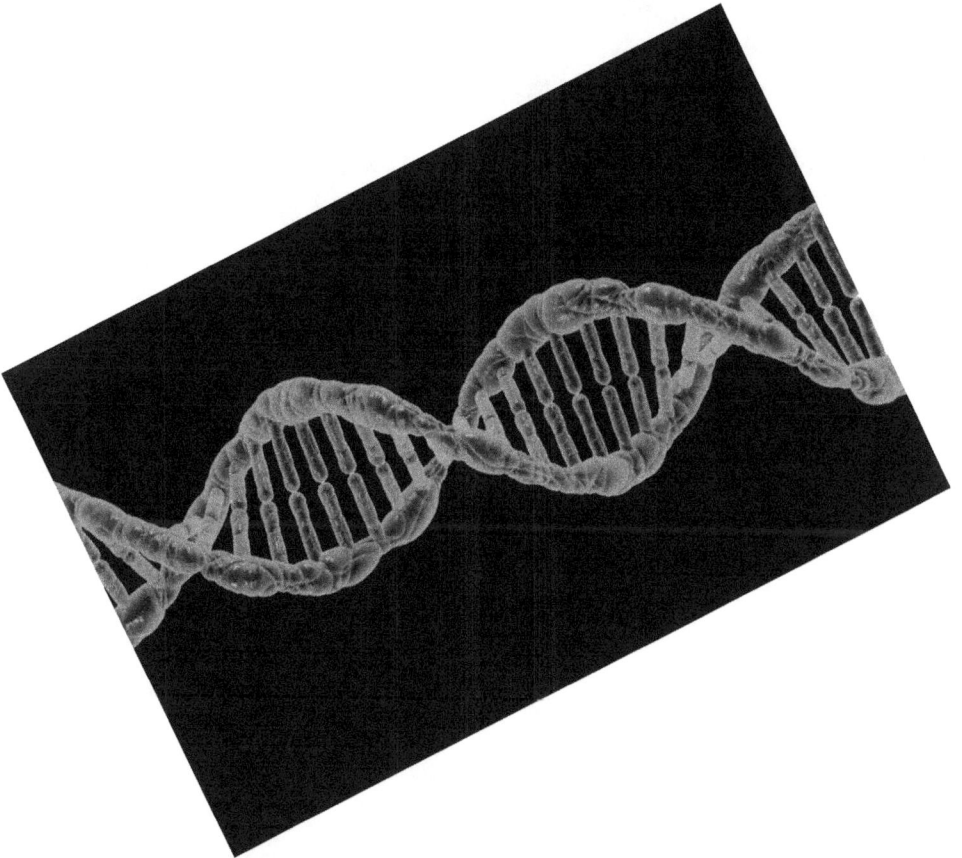

FIDEL M. DONALDSON

CHAPTER 1
DNA: NATURAL

When you examine the earth and its complexities in terms of the planetary system and the various lifeforms such as people, plants and animals, only one conclusion can be drawn as far as I am concerned—that conclusion is this; there must be a creator God. Whether astronomy or biology, the universe and the lifeforms which inhabit the earth, provides evidence of an intelligent designer and that designer is the God of the Bible; the Logos, the Word who became flesh. He is called Jesus Christ, Yeshua. Genesis 1:1 declares emphatically, "In the beginning God created the Heaven and the earth." John 1:1-3 gives us insight into who that Creator God is; "In the beginning was the Word, and the Word was with God, and the Word was God. The same was in the beginning with God. All things were made by him; and without him was not anything made that was made."

To me it is a stretch of the imagination to think that this awesome complex universe and all that it contains are the byproducts of a Big Bang that caused life to start, and evolve from some protozoa to what we see today. If you accept the theory of evolution, then your faith is in man's reasoning and not God's word. Irrespective of how brilliant the mind of the man or the woman is; if their brilliance does not lead him to the conclusion that all things were created by God and He upholds all things by the word of His power, I have to concur with the psalmist who wrote; "the fool hath said in his heart, there is no God" (Psalms 53:1).

Life in The Blood

The human anatomy and its physiology are extremely vast and complex from the cellular level on up. A cell is defined as, the smallest structural and functional unit of an organism, typically microscopic and consisting of cytoplasm and a nucleus enclosed in a membrane. Just look at the organs in the human body and how they function, or examine the blood that runs through the human veins and you will marvel it its complexities. The article titled, *"Blood Basics"* by the American Association of Hematology, gives this definition and function of blood:

"Blood is a specialized body fluid. It has four main components: plasma, red blood cells, white blood cells, and platelets. Blood has many different functions, including:

- transporting oxygen and nutrients to the lungs and tissues

- forming blood clots to prevent excess blood loss

- carrying cells and antibodies that fight infection

- bringing waste products to the kidneys and liver, which filter and clean the blood

- regulating body temperature

The blood that runs through the veins, arteries, and capillaries is known as whole blood; a mixture of about 55 percent plasma and

45 percent blood cells. About 7 to 8 percent of your total body weight is blood. An average-sized man has about 12 pints of blood in his body, while an average-sized woman has about 9 pints." I challenge you to pick any part of the human body and examine its function and you will be amazed how each part or component in the human body is intricately connected to, interacts and works with the other organs and systems, to make the body God's greatest creation. Time does not permit me to delve into the human brain and the absolute wonder that it is.

The Blood of Jesus

The Adamic contaminated blood, transported sin and death to all human beings because of their connection to Adam. In-order to be restored, the human race needed a blood transfusion. Type Rh negative or Rh positive wouldn't do. Not even the universal, O negative or AB sufficed. This blood had to be pure and untainted. There is only one person who walked this earth who had the ability to offer blood that was not corrupted and contaminated by sin. His name is Jesus. Others have come, claiming to be sent by God, but they were born in sin and conceived in iniquity so they were immediately disqualified. Jesus was, is and will always be qualified to save, because of the nature of His Nature. He was God manifested in human flesh; He was Deity cloaked in Humanity; the King of Kings and the Lord of Lords; the Conquering Lion of the Tribe of Judah; the Elect of God, the Ever-Living God.

His sole purpose for coming into the world was to shed His Blood for the remission of sin. He is the only one who can restore wayward children back to their Father in heaven. He is the only one who can remove the word, bastard from the life of a person who is not a part of the family of God. No amount of intellect, no amount of wealth, riches, prestige or good deeds are able to do it. Religious activities, no matter how zealous the practitioner, cannot and will not facilitate renewal and transformation from the Adamic to the Divine. It has to come through the blood and the spirit. People do all kinds of things in the name of religion, but a person who is cleansed by the blood of Jesus and led by the Holy Spirit, will do the things his Father in heaven instructs him them to do. Jesus Christ, the Savior, is the only one who has the power and the authority to do it. Anyone else claiming to have the power and the authority to do it is a usurper, an interloper and a charlatan. Jesus declared, "All things are delivered unto me of my Father: and no man knoweth the Son, but the Father; neither knoweth any man the Father, save the Son, and he to whomsoever the Son will reveal him" (Matthew 11:27).

Knowledge of God the Father, can only come through Divine revelation and not from religious works that produce perspiration but no manifestation. Jesus came to give the Sons of God, a revelation of their Father. (Matthew 16:18)

Revelation begins when there is a washing by His Blood which purges the bloodline and transfers new DNA. Jesus has the DNA or the Divine Nature of Abba because He is God. His Blood is

10

spotless and His life is sinless. According to John 1:29, He is the Lamb of God which takes away the sins of the world. He takes away the old Adamic nature. That old nature separates and blinds the sinner, but Jesus restores and opens the eyes of the new born, so He is able to see through Divine revelation his Father. When a person receives salvation at the new birth, the process of sanctification and consecration starts, which facilitates the dying of the old Adamic nature and the receiving of Abba's DNA. 2 Corinthians 5:17 says, "Therefore if any man be in Christ, he is a new creature: old things are passed away, behold, all things are become new." The renewal affects the whole man. I must emphasize the fact that the process of renewal is not something that is done overnight. Once the baby is born through conversion, a renovation project begins which will culminate in newness of life through a newness of nature.

There is no child that is born and becomes an adult overnight. Jesus, the Son of God went through the process of growth and development like all other babies. He did not exempt Himself from the process. At twelve years old, He was zealous for the things of His Father, but He also recognized and did not circumvent process. In a conversation he had with His mother, when He was left behind in Jerusalem and she and Joseph sought Him sorrowing, Jesus said these words when she questioned Him, "How is it that ye sought me? Wist ye not that I must be about my Father's business? And they understood not the saying which he spake unto them. And he went down with them, and came to

Nazareth, and was subject unto them: but his mother kept all these sayings in her heart. And Jesus increased in wisdom and stature, and in favour with God and man" (Luke 2:49-52). If Jesus grew in such great wisdom and stature, having favor with God and man when He subjected Himself to earthly parents, can you imagine how prolific your growth, development and favor will be, as you continually subject yourself to your Daddy God, and those to whom He has given Apostolic and Prophetic oversight, to aid in your growth and development? It is impossible to grow in wisdom, stature, and have favor with God and man, when spiritual renewal and transformation does not facilitate a change in the nature of a person from Adamic to Divine.

Although the process is gradual, it is sure to produce spiritual fruit if the new convert is nurtured in the things of God. My wife counseled our pregnant daughter to be careful of the types of food she put in her body, because whatever she ate, her baby would eat. Some mothers drink, smoke and do other risky things when they are pregnant and it has a negative effect on their babies. A born again baby who is given the love of fellowship and nurturing through the word will grow into a strong and powerful adult in the things of God and will exude the attributes of a child having the Divine and not the Adamic Nature. You can tell who a person's daddy is by the way she looks and acts.

In a *Smithsonian.com* article, it is reported that "scientists estimate that the human body contains 37.2 trillion cells. These cells are the basic building blocks of all living things." Cells give our bodies structure, they take in nutrients from the food we eat and convert those nutrients into energy. The cell is to the human body what the word of God is to the Body of Christ—it gives the body order and it gives it structure. Groups of cells in our bodies work together to perform specific functions and are called tissue. The Old and New Testament contain the word of God and represent tissue because both Old and New Testament give Divine revelation to the Body of Christ; This Divine revelation aids the body in growth and development—both natural and spiritual. When Ezekiel spoke the Word of the Lord to the dry bones that were scattered; the Word caused the bones to come together. He saw sinews, flesh and skin cover them, but there was no breath in them. The lack of breath meant there was no Spirit in them, therefore, there was no life in them. God told him to prophesy to the wind, and He told him what to prophesy, "*Come from the four winds, O breath and breathe upon the slain so they may come to life* (Ezekiel 37:8-9). Both wind and breath represent the Spirit which gives life and are the building blocks and the sustainer of the life of the body of Christ.

Fundamentals-Deoxyribonucleic Acid

DNA contains the instructions for making all living things. DNA is basically a long molecule that contains coded instructions for the cells. Everything the cells do is coded somehow in DNA — which cells should grow and when, which cells should die and when, which cells should make hair and what color it should be.

Our DNA is inherited from our parents. We resemble our parents simply because our bodies were formed using DNA to guide the process—the DNA we inherited from them. About half our DNA comes from our mother, and half comes from our father. Which pieces we get are basically random, and each child gets a different subset of the parents' DNA. Thus, siblings may have the same parents, but they usually do not have exactly the same DNA.

Nature education's Scitable reports, "Although few people realize it, 1869 was a landmark year in genetic research, because it was the year in which Swiss physiological chemist, Friedrich Miescher first identified what he called, "nuclein" inside the nuclei of human white blood cells.

(The term "nuclein" was later changed to "nucleic acid" and eventually to "deoxyribonucleic acid or "DNA"). Miescher's discovery of nucleic acids was unique among the discoveries of the four major cellular components (i.e., proteins, lipids, polysaccharides, and nucleic acids) in that it could be "dated precisely... [to] one man, one place, one date." In addition, *National science foundation* discovered that: "The DNA stored in the nucleus of a single human cell spans over six feet in length if stretched from end to end. Made up of four chemical building blocks called A, C, T and G, for short. The building blocks link to form the molecule's famous "double helix" structure, which allows genetic information to be copied and passed down from one generation to the next." These four are all that are necessary to write a code that describes our entire body plan. The wisdom given to men by God is breath-taking. The wisdom revealed in God's word is even more exhilarating. The Word of God is such a viable living entity that it can be passed from generation to generation—without losing its ability to have a profound impact on each.

The Creator and His Creation

Notice, there are four major cellular components. Ezekiel was told to speak to the wind that cometh from the four winds, because four is the number for God the creator and His creation. There are four corners to the earth. Four regions: North, South, East and West: Jesus arrived at the gravesite of His friend Lazarus on the fourth day to resurrect Him so the people would know He had power over death. The four major cellular components are one of many examples of the dynamic creativity of God our most intelligent designer.

In 1953 American biologist James Watson and English physicist, Francis Crick came to the ground-breaking conclusion that DNA molecule exists in the form of a three dimensional double helix. The number three plays a significant role in the DNA molecule and it plays a significant role in the Bible and the lives of all human beings. Here are some examples of the prominence of the number three in human life: Pregnancy is divided into three thirteen week parts called Trimesters. The signs of pregnancy are divided into three general groups: Presumptive, Probable, and Positive. After fertilization, a cell is formed called a Zygote. The cells in the Zygote become smaller as they divide and eventually form a solid ball called the Morula which enters the Uterus on the third day. After implantation, the Zygote transforms its embryonic disc into three primary germ layers know as, ectoderm, mesoderm, and endoderm. By the third week the Mesoderm and neural tube form and the primitive heart begins to pump. Each germ layer develops into a different part of the growing Embryo. Three basic stages characterize pre-natal development; The Zygote, the Embryo, and the Fetus. God's unique finger print is all over the design and creation of the universe and all that it contains. Do a geological study, a biological study, and an anthropological study and the end result will be—Yeshua is the intelligent designer and creator of everything that is seen and unseen.

Chapter 2

DNA: IN THE 21st CENTURY

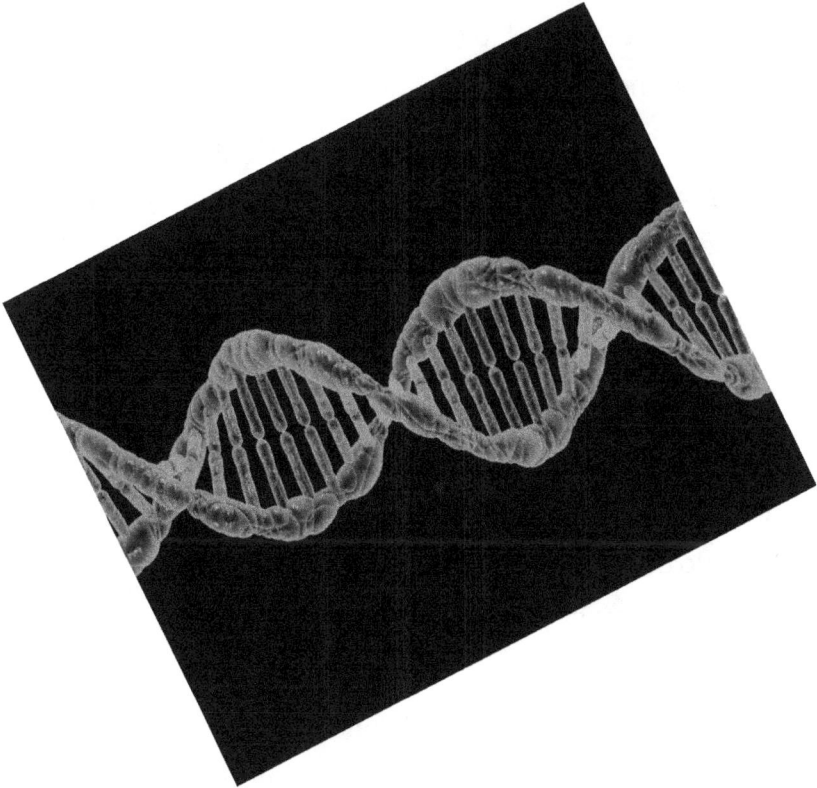

CHAPTER 2
DNA IN THE 21st CENTURY

The letters DNA have become a part of our vocabulary and many people are familiar and even fascinated with the term as a result of television shows like, CSI, Forensic Files and one of my favorites, Law & Order. These shows mesmerize the viewing audience with the solving of sensational and heinous crimes by the use of DNA testing. Prior to the discovery of DNA, fingerprinting was one of the main methods used to convict or exonerate an individual accused of a crime if there was not an eyewitness. Each person has a fingerprint that is unique and not shared by anyone else in the world; even identical twins who share a lot of common traits have their own, individual finger print; unlike fingerprints, however, we share DNA traits with our family members.

Decades after the discovery of DNA, the list of additional uses for DNA fingerprinting continues to grow. For example, DNA markers have proven to be powerful in the study of population genetics. Molecular markers are used to detect sudden changes in populations, effects of population fragmentation, and interaction of different populations

Solving Crimes

With the groundbreaking discovery of DNA, law enforcement agencies do not have to rely solely on a person's fingerprint to determine if they are the one who committed the crime. Wanted criminals have gone to great lengths to alter their fingerprints and their personal appearance in an attempt to avoid capture. A person may wear a pair of gloves in the transmission of a crime, but if they leave a strand of hair, a drop of blood or a cigarette butt at the crime scene, DNA can be taken from those things to prove they were present at the scene of the crime. Prior to the discovery of DNA, law enforcement officials would attempt to get fingerprints from a crime scene in hopes of solving the crime by identifying possible suspects. If no fingerprints were discovered, but investigators had a suspect, they would ask the person to take a polygraph, or what is commonly known as a lie detector test. The problem with a lie detector test is, it is not admissible in court, and cunning criminals have found ways to beat it. However, there is no getting around DNA found at a crime scene because it connects the perpetrator conclusively to the crime. Law enforcement personnel will seal off a crime scene until their forensic unit is called in, in-order to avoid contamination of specimen.

One of the most sensational trials in America was the OJ Simpson trial. Simpson was accused of brutally murdering his ex-wife Nicole, and her male friend, Ron Goldman. The lead detective in that case made some errors, which coupled with some other factors such as widespread corruption and police brutality against the Black Community, caused the prosecution the case. There was a deep mistrust of the LAPD by many in the Black Community. One of the detectives was accused of being a racist and the lead detective was accused of tampering with and contaminating blood evidence. The Simpson case was well publicized because it was broadcast live on television. It was a polarizing case and it exacerbated the deep racial divide that exists in America.

There was a horrific triple homicide reported in the news recently of a wealthy businessman, his family and their maid. The perpetrator(s) of the crime set the house on fire in hopes of destroying evidence, but investigators were able to identify a suspect through DNA testing of the crust of a pizza that was discovered in the home. The brazen criminal ordered pizza, while terrorizing the family and their maid to his own detriment. In the midst of his calculated, thorough effort to eliminate all the evidence, one thing eluded him. He did not realize that his DNA would be found on the pizza crust that he had left behind. DNA testing has revolutionized the field of forensic science and expedited the execution of justice. There are numerous individuals who have spent many years in prison because of a rape accusation until DNA evidence exonerated them. Likewise, many individuals who committed heinous crimes and thought they got away were justly charged and convicted when their DNA linked them to the crime.

With the innovation of DNA testing, the FBI and other law enforcement agencies are able to reopen cold cases that have been unsolved for decades and bring the perpetrators to justice. Many innocent prisoners who were serving long prison sentences, and their families who sacrifice much time, energy and finances for them have rejoiced as DNA evidence was used to set them free.

In an article, *What DNA can Tell Us*, James Randerson explains how DNA can solve crimes; Matching a DNA sample (say from a blood or semen stain) from a crime scene to the perpetrator relies on regions of DNA in between genes that have lots of variability. The technique involves snipping up the DNA using enzymes called restriction endonucleases, which cut the DNA only when they come across a specific sequence. If everyone's DNA were the same then the pieces left after this frenzy of molecular slicing would all be the same length. But there are repeated sections of DNA that vary considerably between individuals. That means the lengths of my cut fragments are unlikely to be the same as your cut fragments (because we have a different number of repeats). By combining several of these variable locations in the genome, scientists can say with very high confidence that a match between a DNA profile found at a crime scene and the profile of a suspect are not the same simply by chance. The probability of two unrelated people having the same profile coincidentally depends on how many variable DNA regions you use, but it is typically one in several billion.

Child Paternity

Another important use is the establishment of paternity in custody and child support litigation. Nowadays, DNA technology is used to figure out who is the father of a child. DNA paternity testing makes it possible to determine a child's biological father to a very high degree of certainty. In an article on CNN.com Jacque Wilson list some interesting things DNA can do.

Map your Family Tree

A $99 DNA test can give you thousands of new relatives; There are Sites that offer to compare your DNA to those they already have on record in hopes of connecting you to unknown branches of your family tree. The test can also tell you your genetic ethnicity.

Solve Ancient Mysteries

No one knew where Richard III, one of the most famous kings of England, was buried until his remains were **discovered in a parking lot** in Leicester. The remains showed evidence of battle wounds and scoliosis, but scientists weren't sure the skeleton was Richard III's until DNA extracted from the bones was matched to Michael Ibsen, a direct descendant of the king's sister. It wasn't the first time ancient remains had been identified using DNA. If it's stored in a cold, dry, dark place, DNA can last for thousands of years. In 2009, a **DNA analysis of some bone fragments** showed two of Czar Nicholas II's children were killed along with the rest of the family during the Russian Revolution, despite speculation they could have escaped. Scientists have even **extracted DNA from**

Neanderthals, who went extinct about 30,000 years ago, in hopes of gaining insight into the development of human life.

Disease Indicator

"The discovery of DNA led to the revolutionizing of the treatment of disease because it holds the instructions for an organism's development, its reproduction and ultimately, its survival." Natural DNA holds the key to understanding how diseases attack and affect the body thus giving researchers the necessary information how to treat and eradicate some disease. The Divine DNA breaks generational curses that opens the door to sickness, infirmity, and disease by giving us spiritual immunization which inoculates and protects the children of God from the sickness that came from the curse of the law.

Predict Future Health Issues

Using **blood from the mother and saliva from the father,** scientists can now determine whether a fetus has any chromosomal abnormalities that could cause a genetic disorder. For example, DNA testing can reveal if an unborn baby will have trisomy 21, or Down syndrome. Researchers are beginning to **expand the field of prenatal genetic testing** even further, using it to identify potential developmental delays and intellectual disabilities such as autism. Genetic testing can also reveal risk factors you may have inherited from your parents, such as a high risk for breast or colon cancer. While this genetic risk factor does not guarantee you will get the disease, it does increase your chances; knowing about the risk may help you take preventive steps.

Help you Lose weight

A growing body of research suggests that our ability to lose or gain weight is shaped in large part by our genes. Scientists have identified several gene variants that may predispose us, and our children to obesity. Rodent studies have also shown that up to 80% of body fat is regulated by our genes, according to TIME.

CHAPTER 3

DNA: ADAMIC NATURE

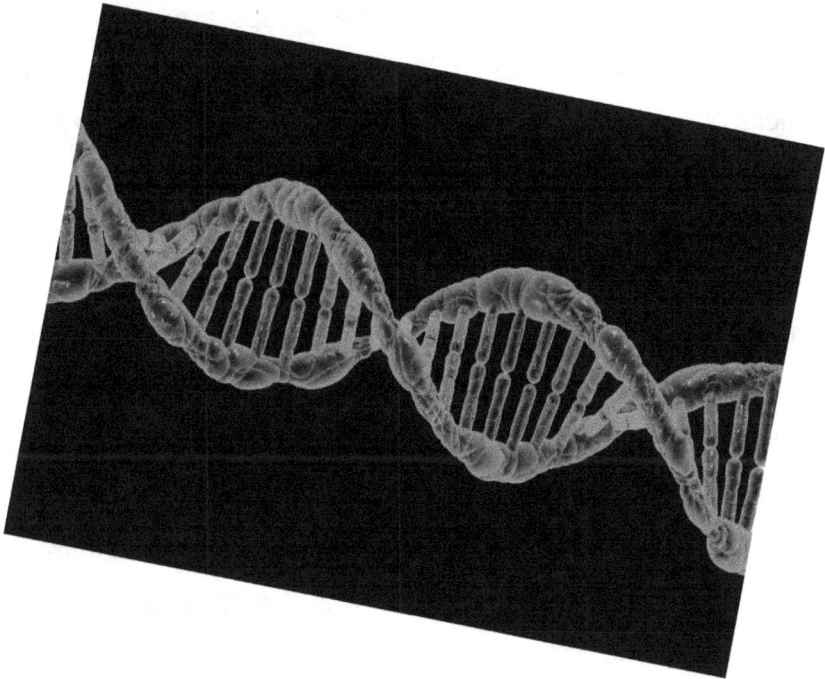

CHAPTER 3
DNA: ADAMIC NATURE

The Adamic nature refers to the carnal or sinful nature inherited from our forefather Adam. The only human being who ever came into the world free of the Adamic nature is Jesus Christ. He was born of the virgin Mary by the over shadowing of the Holy Spirit. All others came through Adam and Eve after they became fallen beings through deception and rebellion. The relation and connection of all people groups are confirmed by Paul's words found in Acts 17:26. "God has made of *one blood* all nations of men to dwell on the face of the earth." The "*one blood*" referred to by Paul, came through Adam and Eve, but unfortunately that blood line was corrupted and contaminated by sin, and that sin tainted the whole human race because the human race is connected by blood. "For the life of the flesh is in the blood: and I have given it to you upon the altar to make an atonement for your souls: for it is the blood that maketh an atonement for the soul" (Leviticus. 17:11).

All human beings are born with a depraved nature. In Psalm 51:5, David said, Behold, I was shapen in iniquity; and in sin did my mother conceive me. Romans 3:23 affirms the depravity when it declares, "for all have sinned and come short of the glory of God;" The Adamic nature is intrinsic and influences our thoughts, actions, and lifestyles. The Adamic nature embodies the works of the flesh as outlined in Galatians 5:19-21; Adultery, fornication, uncleanness, immorality, impurity,

sensuality, idolatry, sorcery, enmities, strife, jealousy, outbursts of anger, disputes, dissensions, factions, envying, drunkenness, carousing, and things like these. Paul warns the people that, "those who practice such things will not inherit the kingdom of God." In Revelation 21:8, John tells the cowardly, the unbelieving, the vile, the murderers, the sexually immoral, those who practice magic arts, the idolaters and all liars—they will be consigned to the fiery lake of burning sulfur.

Deception and Rebellion

When Eve was deceived by the serpent and Adam turned against God, by joining her in doing what God told them not to do, they attempted to cover their nakedness by making aprons of fig leaves from a tree in the garden. I am sure the aprons were beautiful, but fig leaves from the beautiful garden could cover their physical bodies but couldn't disguise their fallen natures. When I think of an apron, I think of a piece of apparel people put around their waist when they are cooking. The Hebrew word for aprons encompasses much more than that. The Hebrew word is *chagowr,* or *chagor* and it means a belt (for the waist): armour, or gird (-le). It comes from the root word, *chagar,* and it means; to be able to put on, appointed, gird, restrain, on every side.

Adam and Eve's nature became perverted as sin entered God's creation and brought moral turpitude, depravity and death with it. They stopped operating in the wisdom knowledge and understanding of God. Although they still had the ability to intellectualize, sin caused their actions to become carnally inspired. With their fallen nature, they responded to the voice of God in a different manner than they did when they had His Divine Nature; Instead of receiving the voice of God with joy in the cool of the day, they hid themselves out of fear. Fear is a spirit that comes from the devil. Sinners are in rebellion against God in their thoughts their words and their deeds so they do everything they can to stay away from Him. However, the problem for them is, He is Omniscient, in that He knows everything and He is Omnipresent, which means He is everywhere. He asked Adam, "where are thou?" but the question was not asked because He did not know his whereabouts, but to get Adam to recognize how lost he had become.

A great deception that plagues many people is the ignorance of how lost they are in sin and the detrimental consequences that will result from it. Most if not all of us have heard stories of people who commit terrible acts. The people who know them may say, "he or she acted out of character." What many people don't understand is this; the perverted nature in a person causes that person to act that way. The person may put forth an image of someone who is morally upright, but the Adamic nature will manifest at some point so the person is not really acting out of character they are manifesting who they really are.

They were probably doing demonically inspired things all along, but were adept at hiding their dark deeds.

Cain and Abel

When Eve conceived and birthed a son by the name of Cain, he inherited DNA from both parents. After Cain, their son Abel was born. Both brothers were born to the same parents, but their futures would be different because one chose to reverence God while the other chose to yield to his inherited carnal nature. Able was willing to submit to the ordinances of God, while his brother Cain acted in ways that were not pleasing to God. As the first born and the older brother he should have been the example of righteousness, but instead he allowed his carnal nature to have pre-eminence. Either Cain was ignorant of the offering that was acceptable to God or he was just rebellious like his father Adam. In either case, ignorance is not accepted and rebellion is likened to the sin of witchcraft (1 Samuel 15:23). Cain brought an offering of the fruit of the ground to the Lord in the process of time. The process of time that it took for the fruit to appear and ripen on the vine should have given Cain the opportunity to contemplate what type of fruit he was going to give the Lord. Would it be one that He would respect and accept or would it be one He would reject?

When the brothers brought their offerings before the Lord; He had respect for Abel and his offering but he did not respect Cain or his offering. The Hebrew word for respect is—sha`ah; it means to gaze at or about; to inspect, consider, depart, be dim, be dismayed, look away. As previously stated, both brothers had the same parents and were brought up in the same home but their encounter with God was different. Abel had a fear and reverence for God which manifested in his sacrifice and Cain did not. That is the reason when God looked at Cain and the offering he brought, there was no respect there. What is God seeing when He looks at your offering? I am not referring solely to the monetary offering you drop in the offering bucket because when God looks at the offering basket in some churches and see the mountain of dollar bills, He probably shakes His head and looks away.

When God examined and inspected Cain and his offering, he became dismayed and looked away because his attitude and his offering were not pleasing. Instead of repenting and getting it right with God, Cain became wroth and his countenance fell, causing God to caution him. "And the Lord said unto Cain, "Why art thou wroth? and why is thy countenance fallen? If thou doest well, shalt thou not be accepted? and if thou doest not well, sin lieth at the door. And unto thee shall be his desire, and thou shalt rule over him" (Genesis 4:6). God revealed that Cain's actions were not well and that is why he was not accepted. A person is truly deceived when they think they can live according to the dictates of a sin laden nature and still be acceptable to God. Cain was told, if he continued not doing well, the door would be open for sin to come into his house. Unfortunately, he did not heed

God's warning, and his anger opened the door that led to the first murder recorded in the Bible. It is interesting to note the fact that the first murder occurred because of the type of offering that was given.

The Hebrew word for wroth is harah; It means: to glow or grow warm; to blaze up with anger, jealousy: to burn, be displeased, earnestly fret self, be incensed, kindle. It is connected to the Hebrew word tacharah; and has the idea of the heat of jealousy; to vie with a rival: to contend. Cain was not glowing or growing warm with love for his brother; on the contrary, he was glowing and growing warm because he was incensed and the embers of the fire of jealousy was kindled in him. The flaw in his nature caused him to look at his younger brother through the eyes of jealousy which caused him to burn or blaze with anger. The jealous fire that was kindled in him, grew to the point where his mind was consumed by a spirit of fratricide. Instead of being a protector and supporter of his younger brother, he wound up killing him. It was the first time a person would kill another out of a jealous rage, but it certainly would not be the last. Since that incident, jealous rages have caused the spurned to kill and destroy many lives. Many of them with the spirit of Cain leading them have taken their own lives rather than face arrest and a trial.

Besides the murder of his brother, the Adamic Nature manifested through Cain in his response to God's question concerning the whereabouts of his brother Abel. His answer to

God's question was— "I know not: am I my brother's keeper" (Genesis 4:9)? Besides murder, we see lying. When a person commits one type of sin, they usually commit another sin like lying, in an attempt to cover the first sin. Cain knew exactly where his brother was because he had killed him. From that point forward men began to perpetrate evil against each other which caused wickedness to increase in the earth. Where does racism, fratricide, the subjugation of women because of their gender, and the enslavement and suppression of people because of the color of their skin come from? They come from the Adamic Nature; they come from the spirit of Cain.

Since the Bible declares that God made all nations of one blood—it means all people groups are related. This should inspire people to love and care for each other, but unregenerate carnal natures cause them to do the opposite. So, instead of working together to make the world a better place, men tend to battle each other for supremacy. Instead of looking at other men as their brothers, they view them based on race, religious creed, and other differences which causes division, oppression, and injustice. I believe Cain knew he was supposed to be his brother's keeper, but the jealousy he felt over the fact that God accepted his brother's offering but had no respect for his—caused him to lash out at Abel in a murderous rage.

The Adamic nature leads to death and damnation. When the Bible states, "the wages of sin is death," and people don't die as soon as they sin, it can give a false sense that sin does not lead to death. What the sinner may not realize is sin causes immediate spiritual death, where the sinner is separated from God because he is in rebellion against God because of sin consciousness; he can have a form of godliness but sin consciousness causes him to deny the power of God, which is the power of the Holy Spirit. The form can take the shape of religious speech and actions, but no true yielding to the Holy Spirit for mind renewal and heart transformation. If you have any doubts about the validity of this thesis, just turn on the evening news and look and listen to what is taking place around the world. You will see and hear about the effects of sin consciousness and the sinful nature of man in the way they interact with one another. From the time Cain killed his brother Abel until now, the moral depravity of man, which is the byproduct of his Adamic Nature, manifests itself in greater and greater wickedness with each generation—the works of the flesh. The sinner ought to be assured that, eventually there is a physical death. "The wages of sin is death" (Romans 6:23)!

I remember a vicar coming to see me when I was incarcerated in England. I was a young convert to Christianity at the time and like other young converts, I had a lot of questions. My born again experience gave me faith in God and His Word and convinced me that His Word is true from Genesis to Revelation. I remember asking the vicar if the story of the flood was true; I believed the story when I asked him, but I was interested in what his answer would be; to my surprise he said it was just a story. If a vicar in the Church of England could say that, then is it any surprise that sinners have not learned from the story of the flood? When man thinks and acts from the Adamic Nature and not the Divine Nature of Abba, the consequences will be the release of the judgment of God in the earth as is recorded in the Bible in the book of Genesis, "And God saw that the wickedness of man was great in the earth, and that every imagination of the thoughts of his heart was only evil continually. And it repented the Lord that he had made man on the earth, and it grieved him at his heart. And the Lord said, I will destroy man whom I have created from the face of the earth; both man, and beast, and the creeping thing, and the fowls of the air; for it repenteth me that I have made them" (Genesis 6:5-7).

Throughout the Bible we see men and women acting under the influence of their Adamic nature. As previously stated it began with Adam and Eve attempting to hide from God, and continued when Cain killed his brother, Abel and lied to God when he was questioned about his brother's whereabouts—One of Cain's descendants name Lamech killed a man; Pharaoh instructed the midwives to kill all the male Hebrew children when they were born—Jezebel plotted to kill God's prophet Elijah—Herod sought to destroy the Christ child, Judas yielded to his Adamic nature of greed and betrayed Messiah. That is just a few examples of the spirit of murder that has plagued the earth since Cain killed Abel; time and space does not permit me to list the many other sinful atrocities by men against other men since the fall of Adam. I thank God for His love and His mercy which stayed the hand of the executioner, so all mankind would not be wiped out because of the bloodshed that seem to increase with each generation. With each generation, men and women become more advanced intellectually, socially and culturally but their depravity seems to get worse, and that is because their nature remains the same—Adamic and not Divine!

CHAPTER 4
DNA: SPIRITUAL

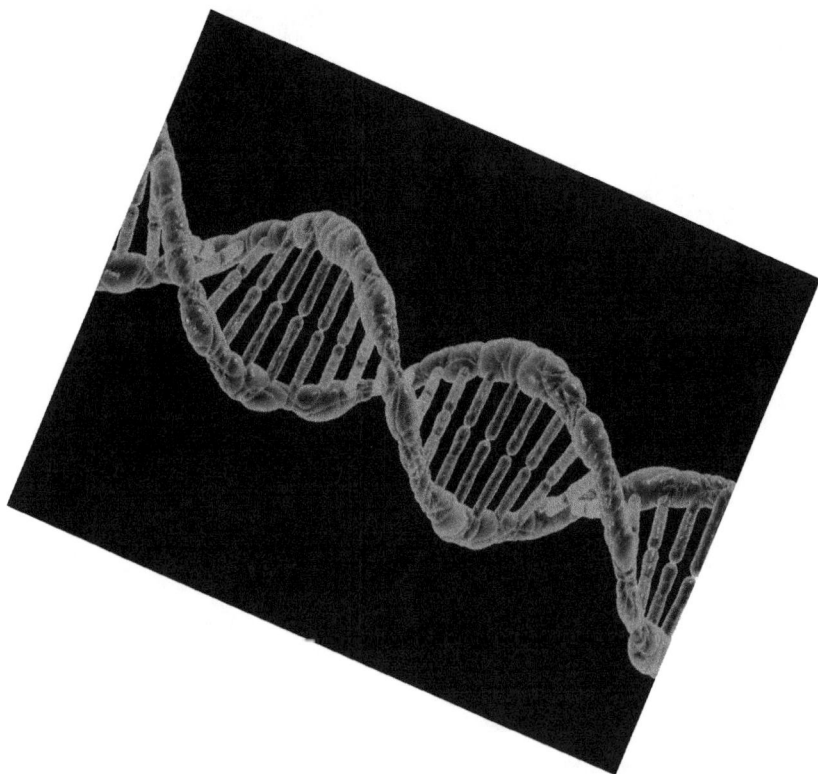

CHAPTER 4
DNA: SPIRITUAL

As previously stated, the purpose of DNA in the cell is the long term storage of information that is vital to the functioning of the body. I was speaking with my good friend, Leslie Minto about the awesomeness of God and His creation. Leslie noted the fact that trees produce fruit at a certain season every year and their leaves change at a certain time every year. Information is programmed into them by God the Creator to do what they do in a specific time and in a specific season. The information is actually programmed and stored in the seed, so when it is impacted by soil, water, oxygen and light, a plant will grow out of it. Eventually, the plant will grow into a fruit bearing tree with each fruit containing seeds with instructions on producing fruit when they are planted and the time and season for growth arrives.

As it is in the natural, so it is in the spiritual. I believe each born again believer has spiritual DNA in them that comes from the Word and the Holy Spirit. The Word contains vital information how the mind, body and soul should grow and develop in-order to live victoriously. The Spiritual genetically programed Word facilitates the growth and development of the child of God, and causes them to produce fruit in their season. Isaiah 61:13 speaks of a people who are called, "trees of righteousness, the planting of the Lord;" a people who will bring Him glory. Psalms 1:1-3 declares, "Blessed is the man that walketh not in the counsel of he ungodly, nor statndeth in the way of sinners, nor sitteth in the seat of the scornful. But his delight is in the law of the Lord; and in his law doth he meditate day and night. And he shall be like a tree planted by the rivers of water, that bringeth forth his fruit in his season; his leaf also shall not wither; and whatsoever he doeth shall prosper." In the parable of the sower recorded in the gospel written by Luke, Jesus likened the Word of God to seed that a sower sowed; Jesus went on to describe the amount of fruit that is yielded based on where the seed fell and the impact of external things, like the lack of moisture and thorns.

The children of God have two sets of DNA. They have the DNA inherited from their biological parents and they have the DNA inherited from God their Spiritual Father through the Blood of Jesus Christ. Their natural DNA for certain characteristics and attributes and so does their Spiritual DNA. Their actions and attitudes depends on the nature they feed. When the Carnal Adamic Nature is fed, they will act like fallen creatures. When the Divine Nature is fed, they will act like their Daddy: GOD! When they feed themselves on a steady diet of His Nutritious Word, and continually yield to Holy Spirit, fruitfulness is facilitated. There is no other way any individual can bear fruit that will remain but through obeying the Word of God and yielding to Holy Spirit. Without the Word and the Spirit, which work in tandem to help the child of God to act according to the Divine and not the Adamic Nature, people would continue to act in a depraved manner.

DNA: Divine Nature of Abba

Spiritually speaking, the letters DNA are an acronym for: The Divine Nature of Abba. Merriam Webster's online dictionary defines the word nature as, "the way that a person or animal behaves: the character or personality of a person or animal: the inherent character or basic constitution of a person or thing: essence, disposition, temperament. When God created Adam, He created him in His Likeness and His Image. The Hebrew word for likeness as it is used in Genesis 1:26, is the word: demuwth; it means, resemblance; model, shape; fashion and manner. It comes from the root word "damah", and one of the meanings of that word is, to think. The children who have Abba's DNA should have His mannerism, should resemble Him spiritually and most importantly should think and act like Him. Thinking like Him is of the utmost importance because an individual who does not think like Him will not act like Him, since thought precedes action.

Since Adam was created in the likeness and image of God—He had the personality, the character, the constitution and the temperament of God. When Jesus was on the earth He had the fullness of the Divine Nature. The apostle Paul confirmed this when he wrote these words to the Colossians, "For in Him dwelleth all the fulness of the Godhead bodily" (Colossians 2:9). Jesus personified and was the perfect embodiment of the full constitution, essence, disposition and temperament of Almighty God, because He was God in human form. Only by faith can the

39

idea of the fullness of the Godhead dwelling in one man be understood. It is not something that can be understood through human intellect and reasoning.

When we look at the character Jesus displayed while here on earth, we can see God truly manifested and dwelling among us. Philippians 2: 6-8, tells us that, although He existed in the form of God, He did not regard equality with God a thing to be grasped, but emptied Himself, taking the form of a bond-servant, and being made in the likeness of men. Being found in appearance as a man, He humbled Himself by becoming obedient to the point of death, even death on a cross—Jesus became a human being so that He could identify with our weaknesses and struggles, (John 1:1,14; Hebrews 2:17; Philippians 2:5-11).

When He walked among the people, the nature of our heavenly Father was evident—and now that He is living on the inside of us—that Divine Nature should still be evident. He was meek and gentle. He lived a blameless, sinless life. He was committed to prayer. He was wise and full of knowledge and understanding. He was obedient to God and to the law of the land. When the Pharisees tried to trick him about paying taxes, he instructed them to give unto Caesar what was due unto Caesar (Mark 12:17). He demonstrated such love. Everywhere he went, he did good. He was full of compassion. He grew in grace and statue. He taught, cared for, and protected His disciples. He forgave and blessed his enemies. When Peter got angry and cut off Malchus's right ear, Jesus reprimanded Peter and restored the ear. He condemned sin, declared the good news, and fulfilled the assignment that he came to accomplish. How wonderful it was, when God could declare in the midst of the temptations, rejection, and persecution that Jesus faced, that "This is My Beloved Son, in whom I am well-pleased."

Jesus was beloved of His Father and well pleasing to Him because He was and is the personification of the fruit of the Spirit as they are listed by Paul in his letter to the Galatians. He listed the fruit of the Spirit as love, joy, peace, longsuffering, gentleness, goodness, faith, meekness, temperance" (Galatians 5:22-23). Jesus Christ is our example, so we must allow the fruit of the Spirit to permeate every facet of our being so God can say concerning us what He said concerning Jesus—that we are His beloved in whom He is well-pleased.

The Breath of God

Jesus Christ came with the fullness of the Godhead bodily to restore to man all that Adam lost. When He created Adam, God breathed the breath of life into his nostrils and he became a living soul which meant he became God - conscious. The breath of God gave him a Divine quality of life which meant he had the ability to live and act in a manner that reflected the essence and disposition of God. Godliness was all he knew because he was placed into a perfect environment. Adam's speech and actions reflected God's Divinity because he was created to be like God. A companion scripture I think fits well here is Job 33:3-4, where he declared,

"My words shall be of the uprightness of my heart: and my lips shall utter knowledge clearly. The Spirit of God hath made me, and the breath of the Almighty hath given me life." God is a Spirit, so when He made man in His image and His likeness, it meant the true essence of man's image and likeness is spiritual. The life, Job is referring to, is the God kind of life that comes through the Spirit. He walked in that life because he was perfect, upright; feared God and eschewed evil. The word for "breath" as it is used in Job 33, is the word, "*neshamah*" and it comes from a root word which means, *Divine Inspiration or Intellect.* The Hebrew word for Spirit is "*Ruwach*", and that is another word for breath: so in essence Job is saying that God breathed His Spirit into him, which is why his words came from an upright heart and he spoke knowledge clearly.

The Spirit of God, the Breath of God, and the Ruwach of God, give you the nature and the mind of God. One of the definitions of the word, Ruwach is to make of *quick understanding.* Isaiah 11:2 confirms this by listing the characteristics and attributes that would manifest in the life of the Messiah through the Spirit: "And there shall come forth a rod out of the stem of Jesse, and a Branch shall grow out of his roots: And the spirit of the Lord shall rest upon him, the spirit of *wisdom* and *understanding*, the spirit of *counsel* and *might*, the spirit of *knowledge* and of the *fear* of the Lord; And shall make him of *quick understanding* in the fear of the Lord: and he shall not judge after the sight of his eyes, neither reprove after the hearing of his ears."

The born again believer who is filled with the Spirit should manifest these seven characteristics of the Spirit. In-order for the manifestation to take place, there must be a continual death of the flesh. When an individual is operating in the flesh there is a quenching of the Spirit and instead of speaking and acting in the wisdom, knowledge and understanding of God, they speak and act foolishly. There is no reason why any of God's children should continue to act foolish when they have Divine Inspiration and Intellect indwelling them through the Spirit. There are times when a child of God will do something that is not orchestrated by the Spirit, but the Spirit will bring conviction, which should teach that person how they should operate. The key is, Christians must be sensitive to the voice of God and obedient to His instructions. Everything that glitters is not gold and everything that sparkles is not a diamond.

In the same manner, not everything that looks and sounds spiritual comes from the Holy Spirit. For this reason, it is imperative that Christians heed the instructions of John that says, "Beloved, believe not every spirit, but try the spirits, whether they are of God: because many false prophets are gone out into the world" (1 John 4:1). When He breathes His breath in someone, they will be enlightened and transformed into the likeness of Christ Jesus.

They will be empowered to live a life that will manifest the Divine Nature of Abba Father through the Holy Spirit. It is worth repeating that Spirit-filled Christians should live lives that manifest the Fruit of the Spirit which are listed above, but they should also exude the character traits referenced in Isaiah 11:2.

CHAPTER 5
SPIRITUAL IDENTITY

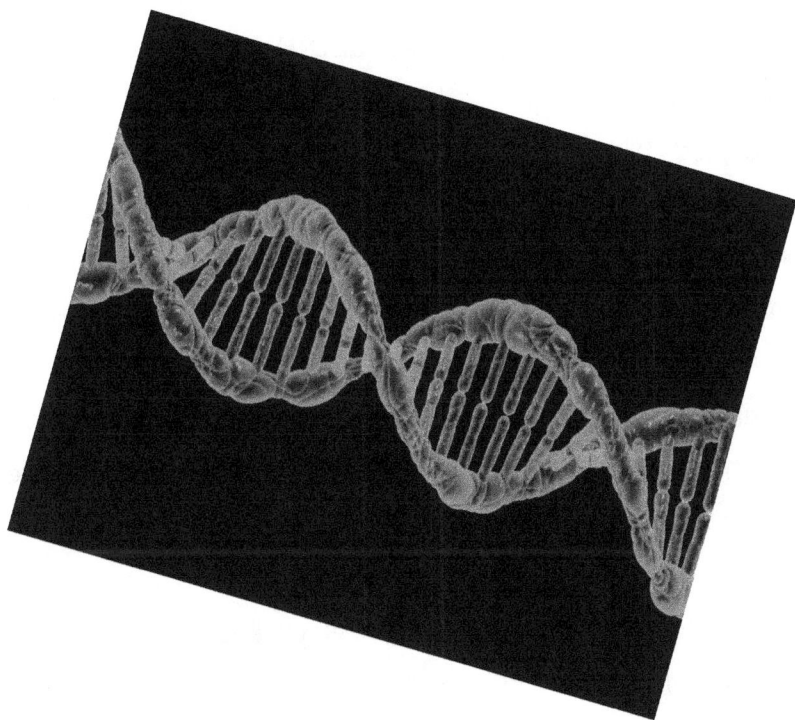

CHAPTER 5
SPIRITUAL IDENTITY

The use of DNA to determine paternity is referred to as DNA profiling or genetic finger printing. It is used to determine if two individuals are parent and child. When a DNA profile is done on a Christian there should be indisputable evidence that he or she is linked to God through His Divine Nature. A natural finger print is exclusive to an individual, but DNA shows a connection to people with whom there is a biological relation. In the case where an adopted child is trying to find his or her birth mom, a maternity test is done. Tests can also be done to determine the likelihood of someone being a grandparent or a grandchild. Not knowing who mother or father is can leave a gaping emotional hole in the heart and mind of a child; that emotional hole can stay with them even in their adult life. All human beings were created with a desire to know how they came into existence. The desire should lead them to seek the face of God, but many use that desire to seek other things.

Jesus leaves nothing to guess work concerning spiritual paternity. Murderers and Liars have a father and he is the devil. James describes God as the Father of lights with whom there is neither variableness nor shadow of turning; John records Jesus' description of the devil as the "father of lies." A person is not a child of God simply because they claim to be or because they have the outward appearance of religiosity. According to Jesus, people can be religious and be children of the devil. Only the people with God's DNA or the Divine Nature of Abba can be called the children of God. The only way to have His Divine Nature is to be washed in the Blood of Jesus so you can be born of His Spirit. Good deeds cannot eradicate the evil Adamic Nature. Fasting, pilgrimages or even praying a certain amount of times during a day cannot do it either. The only way to overcome the Adamic Nature is through the Blood.

In the natural, a woman in a healthy, monogamous relationship, is certain who her child's father is. If she is promiscuous however, there are times when a DNA paternity test has to be done to determine who the daddy is. Not so with the child of God. No one should have to question or second guess their heritage or birthright. His DNA should permeate and saturate them to the point where their connection to Him is readily seen. A particular religious denomination should not be the thing that identifies someone. DNA should be the thing that people recognize when they interact with the children of God. His DNA should be like a light that shines through you that men are able to see and give glory, honor and praise to your Daddy in heaven. When your life is placed under the microscope and examined, the first thing the examiner should see is your DNA. It is the thing that tells them who you are. It tells them who you are related to or connected to. They need to be able to see the resemblance you have to your Daddy. There should be no ambiguity about your true identity, because when you open up your mouth you should have the voice of your Daddy. Your attitude and your actions should reflect your Divine connection to your Daddy. I am always intrigued when I am asked by other Christians, what church I go to. When many of them ask me that question, I know it is a code for their real question, which is, what denomination I belong to. My desire for them is to see the DNA in me and recognize that I am part of the FAMILY OF GOD, a disciple of Jesus Christ, a citizen of the kingdom—an heir and a joint heir with Jesus. In a nutshell, when they see you and me, they should see Daddy.

I remember showing a former co-worker a picture of my son and as soon as he looked at the picture he said, "That is you without the beard." Some people will use the term, "you can't hide" to describe how closely a child resembles their parent. My sister in-law came over for Thanksgiving and the first thing she said when she saw me was, "you look just like Malik" Malik is my son and the resemblance is so striking that she stated it and smiled. On some of the programs on television where there is a dispute as to who is the father of a child, it is obvious that the child belongs to the person because you can see it in the similarity of their facial features. There are some families where cousins look like brothers and sisters because the dominant gene in that family produces a resemblance that is so uncanny. When a child has a parent who struggles with deviant behavior, economic challenges, or character flaws and is not considered a good parent, often times there's a reluctance on the part of the child

48

when they are told, they look like that parent. Praise God, it is not so with our heavenly Father. Since He is perfect in every way, His children love to be compared to Him.

Some children may be ashamed of their earthly fathers because of the lifestyle they live but not so with the children of Father God. His children love to be identified with Him because He is the most loving, kind and compassionate Father there is. He showers love upon His children and when He chastens them, He does it out of love and for their benefit. Some earthly fathers abuse their children, but our Father God has His children's best interest at heart. "For whom the Lord loveth he chasteneth, and scourgeth every son whom he receiveth. If ye endure chastening, God dealeth with you as with sons; for what son is he whom the father chasteneth not? But if ye be without chastisement, whereof all are partakers, then are ye bastards, and not sons" (Hebrews 12:6-8).

Every child should have a father who is like Father God. He is the supreme model of a perfect parent; A model that all earthly fathers should pattern themselves after. Jesus instructed His disciples to, "Be ye therefore perfect, even as your Father which is in heaven is perfect" (Matthew 5:48). When Father God is the model, there will be no child abuse and no child would be left behind. No child would have to wonder, "Who's my daddy." The identity of daddy will be plain for all to see for they will have the Divine Nature of Abba. When I came back to the United States from my time of incarnation in England—my wife told me prior to my return home—when my youngest son saw some men, he would ask her—mommy, is that my daddy? It brings tears to my eyes when I think about it. There are many children who lack self-confidence because they don't know their daddy.

The longing in the human soul can only be satisfied with knowledge of the Creator God. Any philosophy, ideology or substance that is used as a substitute to fill that desire is temporal at best. If the philosophy, ideology or substance is sin laden it will lead to death. For the Christian— God is the Author and Creator of the universe and the life it contains. Psalms 68:4-5 declares, "Sing unto God, sing praises to his name: extol him that rideth upon the heavens by his name JAH, and rejoice before him. A father of the fatherless, and a judge of the widows, is God in his holy habitation." A child who is fatherless or who does not know the identity of his father can grow up with a stigma. When the child goes to school and other children are speaking about their fathers in glowing terms, the fatherless child can feel sad and insecure; When there are activities at school that require the attendance of parents, the fatherless child can feel left out. Thanks be to God for being a Father who loves and cares for widows and orphans. Every child who has to grow up without their father in the home should know they have a Father in heaven who loves them. His desire is that no child be left behind but that all would come to know Him as Abba Father.

He is our Spiritual Father who sets the course and compass of our lives. My first child did not grow with me and I remember the day when she asked me a question that pierced my heart. She asked, "Why did you leave me." I had to reassure her that it was not her that I left. I told her that I was young and immature at the time of her birth and my leaving had nothing to do with her and everything to do with my lack of maturity at the time. There are children who grow up feeling rejected and abandoned and blame themselves for their fathers not being in the home. Although I did not spend the quality time with my daughter that I should have, I thank God for the type of temperament she has, a temperament of forgiveness. It is amazing how forgiving a child can be where an absentee father is concerned. They have such a desire to have their daddy in their life, they are willing to forgive him for the years he neglected them.

The opportunity to connect or re-connect with a father or a mother to whom they have been estranged causes them to forget about the transgressions and misdeeds of the parent who was so addicted to drugs and alcohol they spent more time chasing the next high than trying to spend time with their child. Having daddy and mommy in their lives is so important the child is willing to accept them as they are while they hope and pray for their transformation. There are some situations where a man divorces and remarries and becomes a father to someone else's children. His biological children can struggle when their father leaves the home and they find out he remarries and is taking care of other children. I was estranged from my youngest child for

51

many years because of differences with her mom who is someone other than my wife. The estrangement caused a great deal of heartache and pain for her but once we were reconnected the love for her daddy started to manifest. A child can spend many years away from her biological father but once she has the opportunity to know him she jumps at the chance because there is something special to her about having her daddy in her life. There are some children who don't want a connection to an absentee father because their minds may have been poisoned by their mother.

There are some females who get revenge on the male who left them by inveigling their children to dislike their father. When these females can't find a way to exact vengeance and punishment directly, they do it vicariously through the children. A father's role is very important in the life of a child; it so important that the adults should make every effort to make sure there is nothing that interrupts that relationship. Separated or divorced parents should do their best to put aside their differences in-order to make sure their children have the best opportunity for success. There are times where the chasm that separates the parents of the child is very wide but all attempts must be made to bridge any and every gap that causes heartache and pain for their child. There may be irreconcilable differences that keep the parents from staying together but there should be no difference that is so irreconcilable that it affects unity in parenting. Some children have the misfortune of living in home where their parents are constantly at war.

After a ministry engagement I met a lady by the name of Elaine, who greeted me with a smile and said she felt compelled to tell me her story of the struggles of being a single mother of 4 boys. After a 20-year marriage, a marriage she thought would have lasted forever but later dissipated in December 2008, The night she remembered as being the worst night of her life. You see, that night was the night she was held against the kitchen wall with a hunter knife pressed against her neck in front of her children, the night she thought her life would surely end. Watching her children look on in disbelief, as they stood there in shock with their mouths wide open. Her second oldest screamed and said, "Dad No! If you touch my mom I will have to kill you!" Her life stood in the balance between her son and the man she called her husband who whispered in her ear and said, "just say one more word and I'm going to kill you." The thought of her life being taken in front of her children was the worst pain a mother could endure. She began to pray to God in her mind and from her heart, asking him to let this cup pass from her. And within seconds, he dropped his hands and walked over to the stove and placed the knife in the overhead cabinet and began cooking as though nothing had occurred. She grabbed the children and ran outside and called the police and he was arrested. And it was at that moment she knew her life and the lives of her children would never be the same again.

When parents have the love of God in their hearts, there will be no room for selfishness, anger and un-forgiveness because the Fruit of the Spirit will manifest in what they say and what they do. A parent can be religious and still be unforgiving and bitter but the one who has Abba's DNA will reflect His Attributes. There is no mystery to the equation and it does not take a rocket scientist to figure it out. The Sons of God are led by the Spirit of God!

Counterfeit

Vain religion can masquerade itself to make a person appear to be operating in the Spirit but the discerning mind will be able to recognize the spirit of vain religion that causes a person to operate outside of the wisdom of the Holy Spirit. There are people who are so deceived they think they can live carnally and appease their consciences by doing religious acts. Jesus condemned this pharisaical condition when he declared, "Woe unto you, scribes and Pharisees, hypocrites! For ye make clean the outside of the cup and of the platter, but within they are full of extortion and excess. Thou blind Pharisee, cleanse first that which is within the cup and platter that the outside of them may be clean also. Woe unto you, scribes and Pharisees, hypocrites! for ye are like unto whited sepulchres, which indeed appear beautiful outward, but are within full of dead men's bones, and of all uncleanness" Matthew 23:25-27). It doesn't matter how expensive the costume bought to cover the body or how expensive the perfume bought to give it a sweet scent. When the nature is sin-laden, it gives off a putrefying stench in the nostrils of God. According to Paul, our bodies must be presented to God a living sacrifice that is holy and acceptable unto Him. When our constitution, disposition, and temperament are transformed through receiving His DNA, then the outward man will be pleasing to Him. It is temporal and futile to spend a great deal of time, energy and finances beautifying the outward man when it is the inner spiritual man that will live throughout eternity.

Some people spend untold amounts of money on plastic surgery, expensive cosmetics to cover blemishes and expensive clothing to cover their bodies while neglecting their nature that is defiled by sin. I've seen grotesque images of celebrities and others who have destroyed themselves with multiple plastic or cosmetic surgeries. It is a shame that they did not understand that what truly matters is having a Godly nature. The outer image is not as imperative to someone who is being led by the Holy Spirit. The Bible lets us know that God beautifies the meek with salvation. Salvation starts a process of purification and beautification that works from the inside out, while superfluous and superficial concepts of beauty are outward and external.

The children of God are not perfect but are on a path to perfection so human frailties will manifest at times and that is why the flesh has to be in a state of constant death. There are individuals who like to live as close to the world as they can but still claim God as their Father, but God is not mocked. Whatsoever a person sows, that is what he or she shall reap. Vain religion allows certain individuals to live carnally while claiming to love God, but individuals with His DNA will readily repent when they mess up because they don't want anything in their lives that causes a separation from Daddy. Abba's children know it is not acceptable for them to be, In the church on Sunday, after they have gone clubbing on Saturday, fornicating on Monday, smoking crack on Tuesday, Bible study on Wednesday, cussing on Thursday, and lying on Friday. God's children know that holiness has to be a way of life and that is why they feed themselves on a steady diet of His word and endeavor to spend time with Him through intimate worship so they can know Him in a personal way. He is not an absentee Father and does not expect His children to be absentee children. His children love to be in His Presence because they know His Presence is the place of the fullness of joy. Carnal children want nothing to do with His Presence because they have a different nature. God's children are born again through an incorruptible seed by the Spirit through the washing of the Blood of Jesus an

CHAPTER 6

WHERE DID YOU PLANT THE SEED?

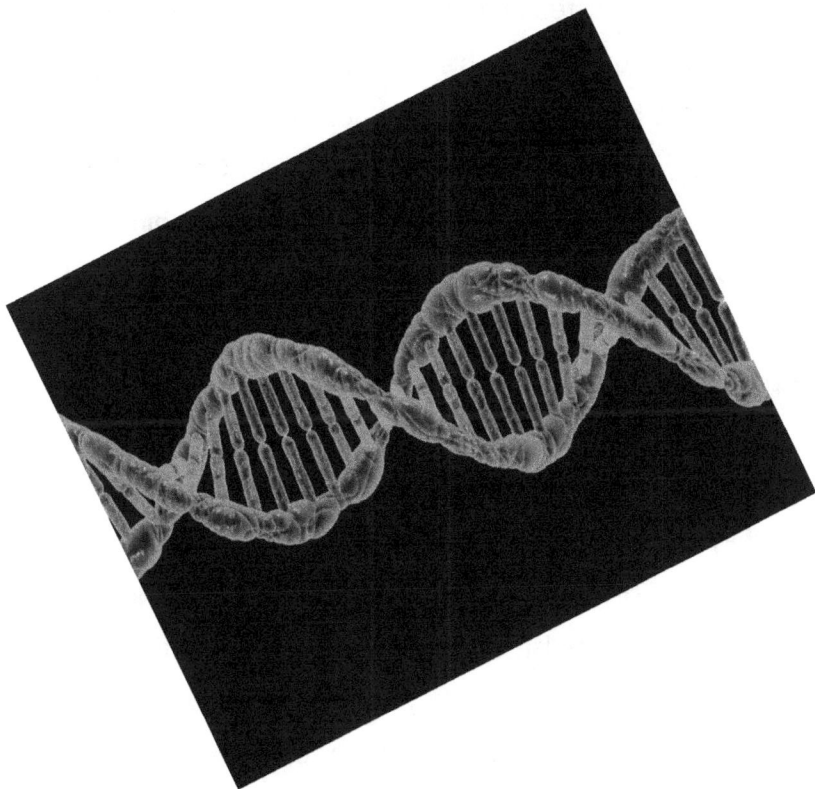

CHAPTER 6
WHERE DID YOU PLANT THE SEED?

Seeds have the ability to reproduce after their own kind. It is an ability that is pre-programmed into them by God. When a seed is planted in good soil it will germinate to the point where it is able to produce a fruit bearing tree. When a seed is planted there is an expectation that at a certain time and season there will be a harvest. Genesis 38: tells us that God was displeased with Onan and slew him because he spilled his seed on the ground. His father Judah instructed him to go into his brother's wife and marry her, and raise up seed to his brother. It was customary at that time that if a brother died and did not have children, his brother would marry his widow and give him an heir. Onan did not want to follow the plan, so he spilled the seed and it cost him his life. In the early eighties and nineties AIDS was an epidemic in the United States and other parts of the world and many people died from it because they put their seed in the wrong soil.

There are women who intentionally choose a male with certain characteristics and attributes to be a sperm donor; a male who they feel have desirable genes that will be passed on to their child. They desire a handsome son or a beautiful daughter who has a high IQ. there isn't anything wrong with wanting your child to be the best and brightest they can be, but at what cost? Some women and some men have no desire to marry but they want a biological child. They desire motherhood and fatherhood without a marital union, so they get the sperm or the egg from the donor of choice and go through the process of artificial insemination. Some women choose a surrogate to carry their child because they have an infertility issue. In some of these scenarios an anomaly shows up in the equation, when the sperm donor decides he wants to play an active role in the life of the child or when the surrogate decides she wants to keep the baby she has carried for the duration of the pregnancy.   There are some lesbian relationships where one of the females is artificially inseminated to bring a child into the relationship and when the relationship falls apart, a nasty custody battle ensues as each person tries to exert their parental rights. For every action there is a reaction and an effect to every cause. Time will reveal the reaction and the effect that will be produced from some of the unconventional lifestyles chosen by people. The beautiful thing about the Born Again experience is this, it has the ability to repair any breach caused in a person's life because of the circumstances surrounding their first birth.

Born of a Virgin

The immaculate conception of Mary and the birth of her son Jesus was a watershed moment in the history of humanity. He is the only person ever birthed into this world without the seed of an earthly father. His mother, Mary, was espoused to a man named Joseph at the time of her conception. He wanted to put Mary away privately, because she was to be his wife and she was with child, even though they did not have intercourse. He wanted to do it quietly, because he did not want her to suffer public shame and ridicule. While he thought about that course of action, he received an angelic visitation from the Angel of the Lord, who informed him that the source of Mary's conception, was the Holy Ghost. I can only imagine the look on Joseph's face when he received that news. The idea of an Immaculate Conception requires faith because it is beyond human comprehension. We live in a world of great scientific breakthroughs and achievements and the idea of a virgin birth is still mind boggling. Joseph accepted the revelation given to him by the Angel of the Lord and took Mary as his wife and became the earthly father of Jesus.

When Jesus grew up and began His public ministry He encountered some religious leaders who were not accepting of His paternity and Divine heritage. During His earthly ministry, His nemeses were religious leaders, called Pharisees and Sadducees. In the eighth chapter of the gospel of John, there is a record of a teaching Jesus did in the temple. It entailed a conversation he had with some Scribes and Pharisees, when they brought a woman caught in adultery to Him and questioned him about what the Law of Moses said, in reference to whether or not she should be stoned. They did this in an attempt to trap Jesus in-order to make Him look like a law-breaker. During the conversation, Jesus told them that He did not bear record of Himself, but the Father who sent Him, bore record of Him. When Jesus mentioned the word

Father, they asked Him about the whereabouts of His Father. He responded by telling them they neither knew Him nor His Father. The conversation heated up, when Jesus accused them of desiring to kill Him. They told Jesus they were not born out of fornication and they had one Father and that is God. Jesus challenged their assertion that God was their Father because of their refusal to accept Him as the Messiah, or the Son of God.

Demon Seeds

The conversation between Jesus and the religious leaders took another turn when Jesus bluntly and emphatically told them, "Ye are of your father, the devil and the lusts of your father ye will do." The Pharisees felt they were close to God because of their strict adherence to the Law of Moses. They looked down on Jesus because He ate with sinners and had compassion on the rejects of society. They were so blinded by their religious piety and legalistic dogma, they could not receive and embrace the fact that Jesus was sent by His Father to seek and save the lost.

A serious blow must have been dealt to their religious egos when Jesus told them the devil was their father and he was a liar and a murderer, WOW!!! I guess it is safe to surmise, if God has children, the devil also has children—When I speak of the children of God and the children of the devil, I am referring to the distinction between people who have God's DNA, through the washing of the Blood of Jesus and the sealing of the Holy Spirit

61

and those who don't. God's Divine Nature allows them to do the works of righteousness.

In contrast are those who I believe have the demonic nature of the devil, and do the works of unrighteousness. When I think about the characteristics of someone who is under the influence of a demonic spirit—I think of someone who is capable of doing evil. Playing out in the news today, are reports of the atrocities carried out by demonically inspired groups, who attempt to spread their poisonous religious ideology through mass murder. These individuals are not operating out of the Spirit of Abba the Father of lights, because if they were, they would spread love, not hatred and murder. Their actions prove they are of their father, the devil, because they are full of lies and murder. If they had the Spirit of God, they would have His Divine Nature and His DNA would motivate them to protect life, not destroy it in the name of vain religion. There have been so called Christians, who have committed atrocities in the name of God but they were operating under a spirit of deception. God told Ezekiel His prophet, "Say unto them, As I live, saith the Lord God, I have no pleasure in the death of the wicked; but that the wicked turn from his way and live: turn ye, turn ye from your evil ways; for why will ye die, O house of Israel" (Ezekiel 33:11)? When God requires the life of an individual, it is because they've not heeded his repeated warnings to repent and turn from their wicked ways. In those instances, His judgments flow from the fact that He is a just and righteous God, not from some insatiable appetite for blood that you see in the demonically inspired zealots and fanatics of vain religion.

Fruit of the Spirit -vs- Works of the Flesh

Individuals who are not converted will manifest the works of the flesh, because they have the devil's dna and his spirit is in them. dna when it refers to the devil and his offspring is, the "devilish nature of anti-Christ." There is a stark contrast between the fruit of the Spirit and the works of the flesh; the difference is akin to the difference between day and night.

In his letter to the Galatians the Apostle Paul wrote about the Fruit of the Spirit and contrasted it with the works of the flesh. "This I say then, Walk in the Spirit, and ye shall not fulfill the lust of the flesh. When Paul uses the word walk, he is not referring to someone taking a casual stroll. The Greek word for walk as it is used there is the word: peripateo; and it means: to tread all around, to live, follow (as a companion or votary): be occupied with. A votary is defined as: a person who is devoted or addicted to some subject or pursuit: a devoted follower or admirer. Someone who is consecrated by a vow. Believers whose lives are hid in Christ are addicted to His Presence, devoted to His Word and have vowed to live a lifestyle of deep consecration. Unlike the children of carnality, they are dedicated to follow the Lord Jesus Christ by living for Him. They refuse to occupy themselves with devilish delights that that cause a breach in the relationship. They know they must maintain a constant vigilance and dedication to the things of the Spirit because of the constant war that is being waged by the flesh.

Paul told the Galatians, "For the flesh lusteth against the Spirit, and the Spirit against the flesh: and these are contrary the one to the other: so that ye cannot do the things that ye would. But if ye be led of the Spirit, ye are not under the law. Now the works of the flesh are manifest, which are these; Adultery, fornication, uncleanness, lasciviousness, Idolatry, witchcraft, hatred, variance, emulations, wrath, strife, seditions, heresies, envyings, murders, drunkenness, revellings, and such like: of the which I tell you before, as I have also told you in time past, that they which do such things shall not inherit the kingdom of God." The children who have the Divine Nature of Abba and follow the leading of Holy Spirit, have a great inheritance in the kingdom of Daddy God. If the children of the devil who have his nature knew the terrible things they will inherit, they would repent immediately and cry out to Abba for the Spirit of Adoption. It is sad enough to see un-regenerated people living their lives as if there is no God, but it is even sadder to see people who project a religious veneer and façade while refusing to submit to the Lordship of Jesus Christ.

Jesus said the Pharisees were the children of the devil because they did not love Him; this leads me to believe when a person does not love Jesus, they open themselves up to being controlled and used by the devil. When a person does not love Jesus they may attempt to live a moral life, but eventually they will succumb to the desires of their flesh. Jesus told them that the devil was the father of lies and He identified them with the devil, because they refused to accept the truth Jesus revealed to them. It is very sad that some people would rather believe a lie than accept the truth. The truth isn't always an easy pill to swallow, but it is the best pill to swallow. A lie may seem beneficial in the short term, but eventually it will be bitter to the stomach. No matter how seductive and enticing the work of the flesh looks and feels, it will always be bitter to the stomach; that is why Jesus told His disciples,

"He that believeth on me, as the scripture hath said, out of his belly shall flow rivers of living water." (But this spake he of the Spirit, which they that believe on him should receive: for the Holy Ghost was not yet given; because that Jesus was not yet glorified) John 7:38-39. Without water, no plant can grow into a fruit bearing tree. Paul went on to tell the Galatians, "But the fruit of the Spirit is love, joy, peace, longsuffering, gentleness, goodness, faith, Meekness, temperance: against such there is no law. And they that are Christ's have crucified the flesh with the affections and lusts. If we live in the Spirit, let us also walk in the Spirit" (Galatians 5:16-25). The fruit listed by Paul should flow out of the lives of all God's children who have His DNA. Remember, they are not perfect, but are on a path to perfection.

There are some individuals who say they don't go to church because there are too many hypocrites there. Here is some food for thought: They don't quit their job because there

65

are hypocrites in the workplace: They don't drop out of school because there are hypocrites in the school system, and they don't stay away from their favorite club or sports arena because there are hypocrites there; Their zero tolerance policy towards hypocrisy relates to the church only and that shows that it is a thinly veiled excuse to continue a lascivious and licentious lifestyle. Hypocrisy is everywhere and to escape it, one would have to exit this world, but a person who exits without the DNA of Abba will wind up in a place where there is nothing but hypocrites and worse.

The Born Again experience does not give Abba's children automatic perfection, but sets them on course for perfection, through a process of purification. As the children of God mature in that process, they grow in grace and resemble their Daddy God more and more, because the fruit of the Spirit will be clearly evident in their lives. There should be a clear distinction drawn between someone who does religious practices, but does not have the Spirit of God or the DNA of God. A person does not have to be a genius to realize that certain trees produce certain fruit. God's children will manifest the fruit Paul listed in Galatians 5 because they have His Spirit. God's children are trees of righteousness who bring Him glory. It is interesting that Paul described the manifestation of the Spirit in terms of fruit production, but the flesh, in terms of works. Jesus spoke about knowing the tree by the fruit it produced.

People will know you as a child of God not based on how you dress or how many scriptures you can quote. Their knowledge of you as a child of God will not be based on your title or how well you can teach and preach; they will know who your daddy is based on the fruit of the Spirit that is manifested in your life. The fruit will let them know you have God's DNA. Paul listed the first fruit as love. Jesus told His disciples, "A new commandment I give unto you, "That ye love one another; as I have loved you, that ye also love one another. By this shall all men know that ye are my disciples, if ye have love one to another" (John13:34-35).

There are individuals from some denominations who try to use religious dogma as a standard or a benchmark to determine whether or not someone is saved and going to heaven. Instead of letting love be the first sign of discipleship, they want to find out what day you worship on, what dietary laws you follow, what name were you baptized in, or do you speak in tongues? The answer to those questions may be important, but what do they matter if the questioner does not have love. The number one attribute of God's DNA is the fact that He is love. Anyone who is a child of God with His DNA, must manifest love. A "love walk" is the evidence an individual has the Divine Nature of Abba. The love principle is so important; Jesus gave it to the disciples as a new commandment.

The Greek word for commandment, as it is used there, is the word *entole*; it means an injunction, an authoritative prescription, a precept. I love the fact that prescription is one of the words used to define commandment. Patients who are diagnosed with certain illnesses are given a prescription by their doctors for medicine that is supposed to help them. They take the prescription to a pharmacist and he or she fills it by giving them the prescribed medicine. God's prescription for the sins that sickens and infects the world is love. His love prescription was given when Jesus' Blood was shed. My scriptural evidence for stating that love is God's prescription for the expiation of sin through the Blood is found in Proverbs 10:12, "Hatred stirreth up strifes: but love covereth all sins." Religion cannot cover sin. Only love can and it does it through the Blood of Jesus Christ. The children of God must endeavor to walk in the truth of His word, no matter the cost. As the world becomes darker and darker and people's hearts become grossly darkened, the children of God must walk in truth and they must walk in love.

I do believe that questions of doctrine and dogma are important, but in their proper perspective. When the children of God are walking in love, which is the first fruit of the Spirit, He will give them the wisdom, knowledge and the understanding of the doctrines of God. When they are walking in doctrinal interpretations that emanate out of the heart of man, they will always put the cart before the horse. Which wise person would put a cart before a horse and say go?

CHAPTER 7

THE JACKET DOESN'T FIT

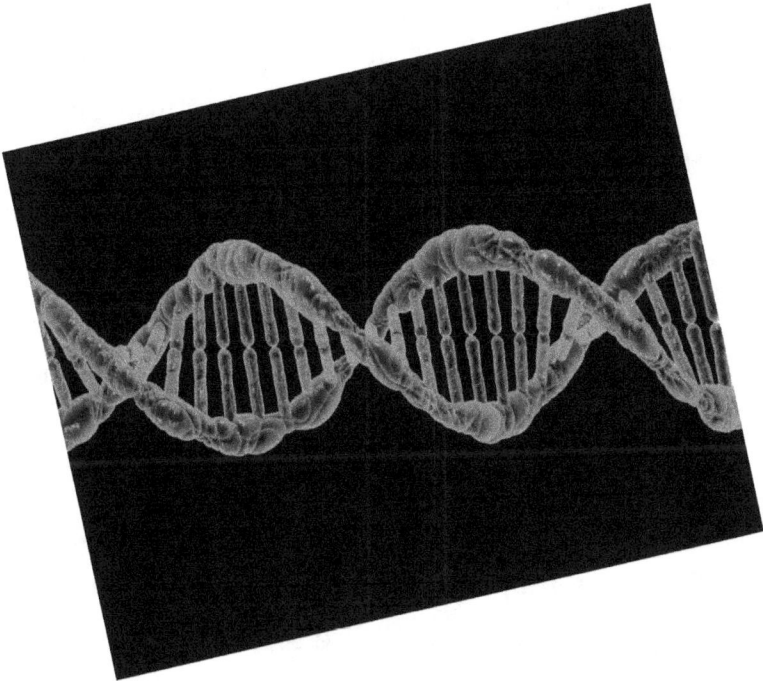

CHAPTER 7
THE JACKET DOESN'T FIT

In Jamaica where I was born, there is a term which no man wants to hear. The term is, "you got a jacket." The term applies to a man who believes he is the father of the child his wife, girlfriend or another woman is pregnant with, but when the baby is born, it resembles someone else. The fact that the child has no features for him or any of his immediate family can cause him to be a laughingstock in his community. In some cases, the mothers are seriously wounded or even killed by the male for the transgression. My wife told me of an incident where a man chopped off the woman's head when he found out the child was not his. The "king of the castle" mentality and the spirit of machismo permeate the minds of many Jamaican men, so when they are embarrassed by being given a "jacket," the consequence for the baby's mother can be very grave.

We're always sure it's momma's baby because she is the one who gets pregnant and carries the baby, but we can't always be sure it's daddy's baby. There are instances where a man has paid child support for years, spent time supporting and nurturing a child he believes is his own, then finds out he is not the biological father of the child. By then, he looks at the child as his own and the child looks at him as his or her father. This new revelation and break in the relationship can be emotionally traumatic for all parties involved. There are some men who have such forgiving hearts, that they are willing to continue to love and nurture the child, as if the child is theirs. In instances where a family is torn apart when a man finds out that the child is not his, the breakup of the family is because the injured party cannot get past the deception.   There are instances where the female sleeps with multiple males and when she gets pregnant, she can only guess who the father is. In most cases, she will give the baby to the person she is more serious about.   When and if the deception is exposed, a DNA paternity test has to be taken to determine who the biological father is.

Over the years, certain salacious television shows pertaining to paternity have become very popular.   These programs portray angry, hurt and emotional individuals sitting on a stage with a host, before an ardent studio audience.   The show's guests usually include a jilted or spurned baby mamma and some dude who refuses to acknowledge the child is his. There are certain episodes, where the child has reached adulthood and after many years, finally get to stand face to face with a man, who has denied being their father all of their life. As the saga unfolds, the hosts welcomes and interviews the anxious mother and the potential father on the set. The vivacious and sometimes belligerent audience cheers and boos, as the mother adamantly tells the male that he is the father of her child while he steadfastly denies it.   The host then uses suggestive, evocative questions, to stoke and fan the flames of mistrust and discontent, in order to whet the salacious appetite of the inquisitive studio audience. As the suspense builds to a crescendo, there are usually several commercial breaks before the results are announced, to captivate the audience's interest and sustain a high level of suspense. Finally, the results are revealed. The host slowly opens the envelope, then announces whether or not he is the father. Paternity is exclusively established, based on the scientific accuracy and reliability of the DNA test. security personnel must be on alert to keep the parties from attacking each other.

As you can imagine, emotions run high on these programs especially at the point where the results of the test are about to be revealed. Once the content of the envelope is revealed, there is jubilation for the female if the paternity test proves the accused guest is the father, and a long, depressed look on the face of the male, once he finds out he is the father of the child he has denied. Likewise, I've seen shows, where the female has to make a quick exit from the stage with tears of shame and disgrace streaming down her face, because the DNA test proved the man she has scandalously accused of being a deadbeat, is not the baby' daddy.

I am legitimate

Miriam Webster's Dictionary defines the word bastard this way, "an illegitimate child." In common English vernacular the word bastard normally refers to a child born out of wedlock. In the Bible the word is used only twice—in Deuteronomy. 23:2 and Zechariah. 9:6. In both instances the Hebrew word mamzere is used. It means to alienate, a mongrel or one who is born of a Jewish father and a heathen mother. The word is very derogatory and can cause a great deal of emotional hurt and pain when it is hurled at someone. Since a child had no control over his arrival into the world and the circumstances of his birth, the term illegitimate should not be applied to any child. Words have power to construct and they have the power to destruct, so it is important that words of life be spoken over every child. A child is a gift and no child should be labeled a bastard or a mongrel. Some children have a rough entry into this world but the manner in which they come into the world should not negate the fact they are special. In a perfect world every child would come into this world to a home with a father and mother who love them, but unfortunately this is not a perfect world and the imperfection can cause great struggles in the life of the child.

I heard a fascinating statement one time; "we are all God's creation, but we are not all His children." Sin caused hatred, lies and other destructive things to soil God's creation, but love caused God to show mercy, by providing salvation, so those who are of a willing heart, can go from being *part of God's creation* to being *part of His family*. When sinners by grace, through faith accept the vicarious and atoning death of Jesus for their sin, they go from being bastards, and aliens outside of the family of God to

73

a position of being a Son. The Sons of God know who they are, and know whose they are. Sons don't suffer from an identity crisis. They don't go through life wondering who their daddy is.

The children of God are persuaded of who they are. They know their inheritance comes through the Blood of Jesus Christ and is based on the truth of His Word. They know that Romans 8:13-15 says, "for if you are living according to the flesh, you must die; but if by the Spirit you are putting to death the deeds of the body, you will live. For all who are being led by the Spirit of God, these are sons of God. For you have not received a spirit of slavery leading to fear again, but you have received a spirit of adoption as sons by which we cry out, "Abba! Father!" Sons of God know their position as heirs and joint heirs, and that Jesus is their older brother. The vicarious and atoning death of Jesus Christ and His resurrection from the grave gives the individual who was separated from the family of God because of sin, a legitimate right to be adopted into that family by grace through faith.

Chapter 8

YOU MUST BE BORN AGAIN

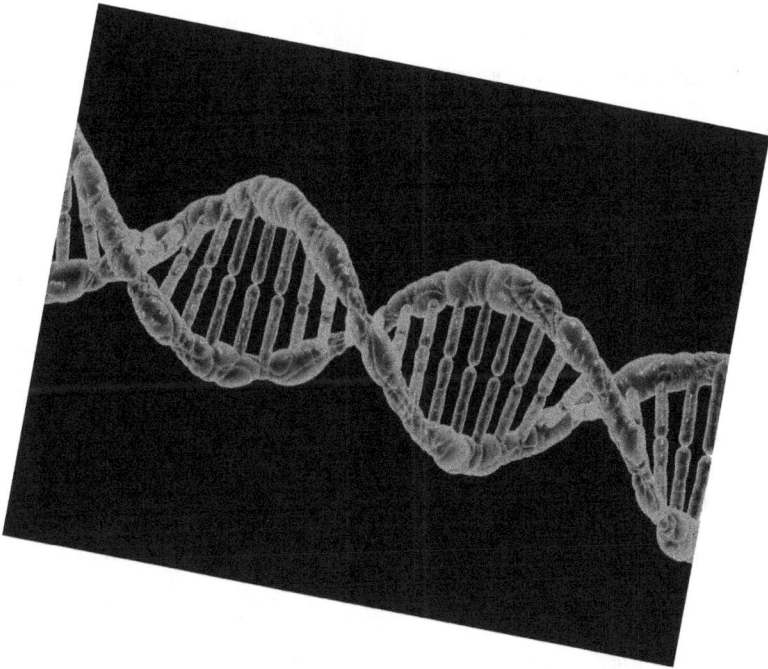

Chapter 8
YOU MUST BE BORN AGAIN

Strict adherence to religious practices does not make a person a child of God. A person can do good deeds in the name of their religion, but that does not necessarily mean he is a good person. I am sure there are Muslim Jihadists, who give alms to the poor and do a lot of the good deeds their Quran instructs them to do. Nonetheless, those same individuals will detonate bombs in public places. They behead innocent people, rape women and kill their husbands and children. Sometimes it seems like radical, fanatical groups like Isis and Boko Haram attempt to see which group can commit the most heinous and reprehensible acts. In spite of these inexcusable acts of terror, they consider themselves saints and martyrs. These individuals operate in the old, sinful, Adamic nature. Unless the nature of an individual is changed from Adamic to Divine, he or she will always revert back to their natural self and that natural self is one of un-godliness.

It is amazing when you compare radical fundamentalism in some Muslims, at least the ones we hear about on the evening news, and a radical Christian. The Jihadist will use a suicide vest to kill people they think are infidels. The Christian has to be willing to give his or her life to spread the love of the Father. When Jesus told His disciples they were going to be witnesses unto Him—He was telling them they had to be willing to be martyred for the gospel. The gospel means good news, and what is the good news—It is that Jesus Christ came into the world to die for sinners. The radical Christian cannot use knives, guns and bombs to spread God's message, they have to use love. The more radical the Christian, the more zealous they are to spread His word, which instructs His children to love and forgive others. The radical fundamentalist Muslim, will kill another Muslim who leaves the faith for another, while the radical Christian prays for that person. That is the difference between being born again of the Spirit and being deceived by a false religious system.

When I refer to radical Christians, I am speaking of individuals who are born of God's Holy Spirit and operating in the fruit of His Spirit. The first fruit of His Spirit is love, so the children of God who are born again of incorruptible seed, show love and not hate. 1 John 3:9-12 declares, Whosoever is born of God doth not commit sin; for his seed remaineth in him: and he cannot sin, because he is born of God. In this the children of God are manifest, and the children of the devil: whosoever doeth not righteousness is not of God, neither he that loveth not his brother. For this is the message that ye heard from the beginning, that we should love one another. Not as Cain, who was of that wicked one, and slew his brother. And wherefore slew he him? Because his own works were evil, and his brother's righteous. John gives the distinction between the children of God, and the children of the devil. He gives the example of Abel who walked in righteousness, and Cain whose works were evil.

For the individual who is not a Christian the term "*born again*" must be a very strange one. Nicodemus was a Pharisee and a ruler of the Jews. Pharisees were individuals who were strict adherents to the laws of Moses. They, along with the Sadducees, made up the ruling council, called the Sanhedrin. From the start of Jesus' ministry, He was opposed by both groups. Nicodemus was one of the Pharisees who was a secret follower of Jesus and came to Him by night. He recognized the fact that Jesus came from God because of the teachings and the miracles which He performed. Jesus instructed him that a man could not see the Kingdom of God except he be *born again*. It is safe to say the term was coined by Jesus. Like many people in the world today, Nicodemus was perplexed by Jesus' revelation. In John 3, He asked Jesus how a man could be born when he is old and how could he enter into his mother's womb a second time. It is evident Nicodemus was thinking about a natural birth, when Jesus was teaching a spiritual principle.

Jesus gave him more detail on the *born again* phenomena, when He told him it was through the water and the Spirit that a man could be born again and have access to the Kingdom of God. Our first birth came through human agents and gave us entrance into the earth realm, but the new or second birth has to come through the Spirit, because Father God dwells in the spiritual realm and that realm cannot be accessed or entered, through the flesh. Jesus went on to tell Nicodemus that things which are born of the flesh are flesh and things that a born of the spirit are spirit.

In other words, the flesh cannot receive and discern the things of the spirit because spiritual things are discerned spiritually. With that revelation from Jesus we understand, there are individuals like the Pharisees who are religious, yet fleshly or carnal.

A person who is not born of the Spirit will never know the deep things of God. He or she may know of God based on things they have read or heard but to truly know Him and have access to His Kingdom, they must be born of the Spirit. If the concept of the new birth was so difficult for an individual of Nicodemus' stature, then how difficult do you think it will be for others who are unwilling to submit to the Lordship of Jesus. The Pharisees were well learned and versed in the letter of the law, but not many of them were proficient in spiritual things. That is why, instead of embracing the ministry of Jesus, they persecuted Him. Some people will criticize and attempt to tear down something they don't understand because they feel it is a threat.

The best thing to happen to me during my time of incarceration, was the day I found a small Gideon Bible in a dresser draw in my cell, and I started reading it. I will never forget the day in March 1991 when my life was radically transformed while reading the book of John. In chapter five—one particular verse pricked my heart, and provoked me to cry out to God for mercy. These words were spoken by Jesus during an encounter he had with some Pharisees. They were challenging Jesus's claim and assertion that He was doing the work that God, His Father sent Him to do. Jesus told them, *"Search the scriptures; for in them ye think ye have eternal life: and they are they which testify of me. And ye will not come to me, that ye might have life"* (John 5:39-40). That scripture turned my world upside down as I sat in the prison cell, because it spoke directly to my heart. It was as if Jesus had an audience of one and that one was me; His words pierced my heart and I knew I had to make a decision.   I knew I did not have eternal life, because when my wife would encourage me to surrender my life to Jesus, my response to her was, "get out of here with that white man's religion, fools go to church on Sundays." I never searched the scriptures, because I was too busy enjoying the pleasures of sin which only last for a season. The season ended when I was locked in a small prison cell facing years in prison. I knew if I was going to be restored to my family and develop the discipline to turn away from the life of sin that led me to prison I had to have the eternal life Jesus spoke to the Pharisees about. I surrendered my heart and my will to Him that day, when I asked Him to forgive me of my sins and they were many. I cried out to Him to cleanse me with His Blood. That is the moment when my new life in Jesus began. It was the moment when old things passed and all things became new. With the help of the Holy Spirit I gained greater understanding of God as a loving Father, and not some distant deity.

Regeneration

God is merciful and longsuffering in that He gives us the process of time to prepare ourselves to be an acceptable and delightful offering unto Him. If our attitudes and our actions are to be acceptable unto God we have to go through a mental metamorphosis Paul gives us the instructions we can follow to complete the process "I beseech you therefore, brethren, by the mercies of God, that ye present your bodies a living sacrifice, holy, acceptable unto God, which is your reasonable service. And be not conformed to this world: but be ye transformed by the renewing of your mind, that ye may prove what is that good, and acceptable, and perfect, will of God" (Romans 12:1-2).

The centurion Cornelius, is a great example of a holy vessel who gives God an acceptable offering. "There was a certain man in Caesarea called Cornelius, a centurion of the band called the Italian band, a devout man, and one that feared God with all his house, which gave much alms to the people, and prayed to God always. He saw in a vision evidently about the ninth hour of the day an angel of God coming in to him, and saying unto him, Cornelius. And when he looked on him, he was afraid, and said, what is it, Lord? And he said unto him, Thy prayers and thine alms are come up for a memorial before God" (Acts 10:1-4).

As we saw with Cain, your offering is an indicator and a reflection of your nature. What you offer is indicative of who you are. The quality and substance of your sacrifice reveals your heart and authentic nature. This is why Paul beseeches the New Testament believer to offer their bodies a living sacrifice, which is holy and acceptable unto God. Their prayers, praise and worship should emanate from a holy vessel, so they can be acceptable to God. Sin causes a separation between people and God the Father. When God called for Adam in the garden, instead of running to God like he usually did, Adam ran and hid. He was suddenly fearful and anxious, realizing that he had disobeyed God's instructions. He knew something was wrong and he knew there would be consequences. He was afraid and felt unworthy to fellowship with God. On page 43 of his book titled, *The Character of God: Discovering The God Who Is.,* R.C Sproule wrote, "There are those who hate God's presence because they cannot stand His gaze. But for those who love His appearing, the presence of God is like soothing music." I love to put it this way—Some people want His *Presents,* but don't want to live a consecrated life that allows them to be in His *Presence*.

To the child of God who has His DNA and is yielded to His Spirit, God's voice is a soothing joyful sound. The psalmist declared, "Blessed is the people that know the joyful sound: they shall walk, O Lord, in the light of thy countenance" (Psalms 89:15). Countenance there, speaks of a turning of the face. When the face of God is turned towards you, it causes the light of His Glory to light your path. When sin causes His Face to be hid, then the path becomes dark.

His Voice instructs His children to think and act by Divine Inspiration. When sin is in the heart, the minds of sinners are perverted and that perversion affects the eye and the ear gate; they become fearful of the Voice of God because they know God is Holy, so they don't want to be near Him. When Jesus Christ came into the world He came as the Light of the world but everyone does not want the Light. Their rejection of the Light will cause condemnation to come upon them. Jesus declared, "And this is the condemnation, that light is come into the world, and men loved darkness rather than light, because their deeds were evil. For every one that doeth evil hateth the light, neither cometh to the light, lest his deeds should be reproved. But he that doeth truth cometh to the light, that his deeds may be made manifest, that they are wrought in God" (John 3:19-21).

His vicarious and atoning death and His resurrection from the grave meant that human beings could be transformed through the renewing of their minds. Instead of having a nature or a natural mind and body that are enslaved to dark thoughts and dark deeds; the new man is partaker of God's DNA. With His DNA comes God's Character, Personality, Essence, Disposition and Temperament. The metamorphosis or transformation can only take place through the knowledge of God given to us by the finished work of the Lord Jesus Christ. The Apostle Peter confirms this when he wrote, "Grace and peace be multiplied unto you through the knowledge of God, and of Jesus our Lord, According as his divine power hath given unto us all things that pertain unto life and godliness, through the knowledge of him that hath called us to glory and virtue: Whereby are given unto us exceeding great and precious promises: that by these ye might be partakers of the divine nature, having escaped the corruption that is in the world through lust" (2 Peter 1:2-4). Lust does not only mean having an

83

overwhelming desire for something sexual. It means a longing or a desire for something that is forbidden. I believe that is what happened to Eve in her encounter with the serpent. I believe when he told her that if she ate of the fruit her eyes would be opened and she would be as gods, knowing good and evil. At some point in the conversation she made up her mind to eat of the fruit. The Bible declares, "And when the woman saw that the tree was good for food, and that it was pleasant to the eyes, and a tree to be desired to make one wise, she took of the fruit thereof, and did eat, and gave also unto her husband with her; and he did eat" (Genesis 3:6). Ungodly desires will cause a person to take things that are not given to them; it will make them take things they are told to stay away from. Many of us can say, "Been there, done that."

One of the greatest deceptions perpetrated by the devil on human beings is fooling them into thinking they can sin with impunity, which means freedom from punishment. The serpent painted a rosy picture to Eve in-order to deceive her into thinking God was withholding something good form her. He didn't tell her what the consequences would be once she did it. Adam knew because God gave him a command not to eat of the fruit and told him what the consequences would be and I guess he failed to inform Eve. Wives make sure you are fully informed and compliant to the instructions God gives you and your husband.

Adamic and Edenic

An unregenerate man has evil imagination and thoughts which causes him to do wicked things. It does not matter how educated, how wealthy or how influential he is. If his life is not transformed by the renewing of his mind through the cleansing by the Blood of Jesus and the indwelling of the Holy Spirit; he will always exhibit a propensity and a proclivity for sin. Transcendental meditation cannot renew his mind by giving him a new nature. Social scientist will always debate about what has the greatest effect on the life of an individual; is it nature or is it nurture? There is a correlation between the environment an individual is born and grows up in and what type of person they become, but environments are created by people and not vice versa.

When God placed Adam and Eve in the Garden of Eden the environment was good because it was created by God. At that time, they had what is commonly referred to as the *"Edenic Nature, which means,* paradisiac, of or pertaining to Eden; characteristic of Eden."* Sin not only perverted the nature of Adam, Eve and every person who would come into the earth through them, it also polluted the idyllic paradise which God made for them. People aren't inherently wicked because they are in the world; wickedness and evil are in the world because people are there. I am not negating the fact that there is some good in the world because there are some people who do good; my thesis is this—while an individual can do good because he or she is taught to do so, the natural propensity and proclivity of all human beings is ungodliness because of the Adamic Nature.

When an individual receives salvation through the *born again* experience, a battle rages inside as the Holy Spirit takes them through the sanctification process. In the letter to the Church at Rome, the apostle Paul succinctly expounds on the principles of justification by faith and the spiritual verses the carnal nature. In Romans Chapter seven, he talks about how God's law reveals sin, and the struggle within. In Chapter eight, he deals with the fact that the Holy Spirit frees us from sin. Here is what Paul wrote, "And I know that nothing good lives in me, that is, in my sinful nature. I want to do what is right, but I can't. I want to do what is good, but I don't. I don't want to do what is wrong, but I do it anyway. But if I do what I don't want to do, I am not really the one doing wrong; it is sin living in me that does it. I have discovered this principle of life—that when I want to do what is right, I inevitably do what is wrong. I love God's law with all my heart. But there is another power within me that is at war with my mind. This power makes me a slave to the sin that is still within me. Oh, what a miserable person I am! Who will free me from this life that is dominated by sin and death? Thank God! The answer is in Jesus Christ our Lord. So you see how it is: In my mind I really want to obey God's law, but because of my sinful nature I am a slave to sin (Romans 7:18-25 NLT).

Paul is saying that a person may have it in their mind to be obedient to the things of God, but the sinful nature, that is within, enslaves and traps them; it keeps them chained to ungodly actions. A slave is someone who is under the control of another. Satan is the slave master for all sinners. Jesus Christ is the only one who has the power to free the slave from the bondage of a sinful nature. It takes blood to expiate sin and the only blood capable of doing that is the Blood of Jesus. According to Paul, sin dominates the life of the sinner, leads to spiritual death, and eventually leads to physical death.

A slave master dominates the life of his slaves by controlling their actions. To control their actions, he must first take control of their minds. The devil controls the minds of his slaves through lustful thoughts and desires. Paul referred to the power within that was at war with his mind. The child of God endeavors to have a mind that is led by His Spirit and that mind is at war with the power of demonic thoughts that constantly attack the mind of the child of God through fiery darts. There is no mental war for the slave because he or she has a nature and a mind that is enslaved, so it is under the control of the devil. He knows exactly what to present to the carnal mind to keep it enslaved to sin. He is not able to totally dominate the will of the slave because they can choose to serve God if they want to, but they are so deceived by the devil, they choose lustful and sensual desires over holiness and righteousness. Sin not only enslaves the nature of the sinner, but it also blinds his mind. With the blinders placed over his mind's eye, he is not able to see the wretchedness of his nature and he certainly cannot see the beauty of the Divine Nature of Abba.

I can speak from first person experience of the blindness caused by the carnal nature. Prior to my conversion in the English prison, I found myself in clubs and parties drinking and having revelry, weekend after weekend. I had a loving beautiful wife at home, but was not satisfied because lustful desires kept dragging my mind into sin laden thoughts. Once my mind submitted, then my body was powerless to resist because it willingly did what my mind told it to do. My wife prayed for me and encouraged me to surrender to Jesus and live a righteous life, but I would always heed the dictates of my carnal mind; that is until the prison door slammed and I found myself in a place and situation where I had to cry out to God.

A New Blood Line: A New Identity

"Therefore if any man be in Christ, he is a new creature: old things are passed away; behold, all things are become new" (2 Corinthians 5:17). When a child is born into this world, she does not have the luxury of choosing the type of family she is related to. That choice is made for her by the two people who decided to come together for a time of sexual intimacy. Some children have the blessing of being born into a family that is wealthy and some have the misfortune of being born into a family that is impoverished. There are no perfect families on the earth, but I believe we can all agree that some families have more problems than others. A wealthy family for instance, has the resources to deal with the problems money can solve. If the child of a wealthy family gets sick or gets in trouble with the law, she can get the best medical care or the best defense money can buy. The person whose family is in poverty, does not have that luxury and must depend on public hospitals and court appointed lawyers. Rich and poor alike are pre-disposed to the DNA or the genes that link them to the particular family into which they were born. There are people in the world who are described as "blue bloods"

because they were born into a royal family. Children born to wealthy or royal families can struggle just like children born to poor families, but in many instances, the struggles are different. Wealthy children may be spoiled and have a sense of entitlement or they may struggle to live up to the family name, but they certainly don't struggle with going to bed hungry and they certainly don't have to wear hand me downs and share a room with one or more siblings.

Many people in wealthy and poor families struggle in life because they grow up in an abusive family or a family with a pre-disposition to, incest, alcoholism, drug addiction or some other activity that causes a great deal of heartache and pain. If they are not cautious, they too will fall victim to the identical strongholds. We see destructive patterns perpetuated from one generation to another. We see the daughter of a teenage mom, also giving birth at a young age. The circumstances surrounding the death of Whitney Houston and her daughter were almost identical. Ms. Houston had fame and fortune, but the fame and the money could not insulate her from addiction to drugs and alcohol. Her death by drowning in a bathtub due to intoxication did not cause her daughter to stop abusing drugs and alcohol. The irony is this; Ms. Houston grew up singing in church. It is not enough to be in the church, we must be the church: the *ecclesia*, the ones who are called out of darkness into the marvelous light of the Father of lights.

Like Father—Like Son?

In Genesis, chapters 20 and 26, we see Abraham and His son Isaac, committing the same offense by lying about their wives' true Identity. It takes the Blood to purify and annul the bloodline and generational strongholds. The individual who is in Christ becomes a new creature. She experiences the second birth. Unlike her first birth, when she repented of her sins and expressed faith in Jesus Christ, she chose to become a part of the family of God. The choice first was made by God, to give her an awareness of her sins through conviction, and to give her an awareness that salvation was available, but she had to make the choice to accept it. It is unlike the first birth, where it was completely up to the parents and not the child. With the new birth comes a new blood line, a new name, and a new identity. The new child of God becomes part of a royal family. The newborn, who comes into God's Royal Family, must be fed a steady diet of the milk of the Word of God.

Michai

My daughter gave birth to a son she named Michai, three days shy of the baby being in her womb for six months. He had to spend several months in the intensive care unit of a pediatric hospital, which specializes in taking care of babies who are born pre-mature. He had to have constant monitoring because he came out of his mother's womb before the nine-month cycle was finished. He had to have help breathing because his lungs were not developed to the point where he could breathe on his own. His tiny body had to have surgery, because he had a heart murmur that needed to be closed. He received his nourishment from an IV because he could not get mother's milk. I noticed, that once he was able to be fed his mother's milk, his growth and development increased rapidly. Mother's milk has the nutrient a baby needs for their growth and development. One of the titles of Father God is El-Shaddai. The Parent Company expounds on the title in an article— "El-Shaddai means God Almighty. El points to the power of God Himself. Shaddai seems to be derived from another word meaning breast, which implies that Shaddai signifies one who nourishes, supplies, and satisfies. It is God as El who helps, but it is God as Shaddai who abundantly blesses with all manner of blessings."

In the same manner that mother's milk is the best nourishment for her new born child, so the milk of the word from El-Shaddai is the best nourishment for the newborn child of God, until he or she can graduate to eating and digesting the strong meat of His word. In His infinite wisdom, He knew the Kairos or opportune time for the new baby to be born into His royal family. God's newborn babies never arrive too early or too late because, "He's an on-time God." When a baby is born, a birth certificate with the baby's name and other pertinent information is issued. When a baby comes into the royal family of God through the new birth, his or her name is written in the Lamb's Book of Life. In His book, the new name distinguishes and differentiates them from the person they were, and the name they were given, when they had their first birth to earthly parents. The born again child of God is an overcomer, because they have crossed over from death to life, through the washing of the Blood of Jesus. "He that hath an ear, let him hear what the Spirit saith unto the churches; To him that overcometh will I give to eat of the hidden manna, and will give him a white stone, and in the stone *a new name* written, which no man knoweth saving he that receiveth it" (Revelation 2:17). In another part of his letter John wrote, "And they overcame him by the blood of the Lamb, and by the word of their testimony; and they loved not their lives unto the death" (Revelation 12:11).

People who are born into earthly royal families have *blue blood*, but people who are born into God's royal family have the *Blood of the Lamb*. Blue bloods have wealth, prestige and pedigree through their blood line, but the prestige and status enjoyed by their family for generations through their blood line is powerless to overcome sin and death. Their blood allows them to be royal where men are concerned but it has no power to transform, restore, or deliver. The Blood of Jesus, who is the King of Kings, and the Lord of Lords is the true Blood of royalty which sets the royal family of God apart from all earthly royal families. His royal family is greater than any earthly royal family, because His royal family is one that is being perfected to carry His glorious DNA or the Divine Nature of Abba. Earthly royal families have great honor and respect in the earth realm, but they have their issues and limitations. Their lineage, though it may be illustrious, is a carnal, fleshly one, whereas the royal family of God is a spiritual one; Jesus told Nicodemus, "That which is born of the flesh is flesh; and that which is born of the Spirit is spirit" (John 3:6).

When a spiritual DNA test is done on you, the child of God to determine paternity, the Divine connection is evident. There is a blood component and there is a spiritual component that confirms the Divine connection to Abba Father. The test reveals conclusively, that you are a son of God. Whether male or female, it does not matter, because Abba has male sons and He has female sons. Sonship is not based on gender, it is based on spiritual renewal and transformation, which comes through the washing of the Blood of Jesus and the sealing of the Holy Spirit. "And there are three that bear witness in earth, the spirit, and the water, and the blood: and these three agree in one" (1 John 5:8). Jesus' Blood is the only agent that can expiate and propitiate sin,

93

so it does not remain as an obstacle of separation, between the sinner and God. His Blood can do that, because it is not tainted by the sin of Adam. Once the new born is washed in the blood of Jesus, the Holy Spirit seals them unto the day of redemption, and becomes the indwelling Teacher, Comforter, and Guide into all things pertaining to the Kingdom. The new born is not made perfect at the time of salvation because there is a process she has to go through for purification.

When the adversary or some demon attempts to accuse them, they can plead the Blood against them in the boldness of the Spirit. The spiritual New Born has the authority to let every demonic spirit know, they are a new creature in Christ, who is born of His Spirit, washed in His Blood, and has a heavenly Father who rules and reigns supreme; a heavenly Father who forgave their sins, past, present and future, because of the finished work of Jesus Christ. He is a heavenly Father who never abuses His children, but always gives them the best. When He chastens them, He does it out of love in-order to bring them back to a path of righteousness.

The royal family of God will have a glorified body one day that has no pre-disposition to addictive behaviors or life threatening diseases, based on a genetic DNA profile from an earthly family with a tainted blood line. The glorified body will be disease free because it will be completely sin free. There will be no need for surgery to remove a cancerous body part or to transplant a heart, lung or a kidney because of failure. There will be no need for DNA testing to determine paternity or the isolation of certain Genes to find a cure for cancer or some other life threatening disease because the born again glorified body will attain a state of sinless perfection. While we are in our earthly bodies, we have to deal with certain diseases; some of them we are genetically pre-disposed to because of our family DNA. That pre-disposition, causes some people to take pre-emptive actions, in hopes of avoiding certain life threatening diseases which come down through the blood line of their families.

Pre-Disposition: Not Blue Jeans but New Genes

An On-line article from *Genetics Home Reference: Our guide to understanding genetic conditions* gives this information about genetic pre-disposition: "A genetic predisposition (sometimes also called genetic susceptibility) is an increased likelihood of developing a particular disease based on a person's genetic makeup. A genetic predisposition results from specific genetic variations that are often inherited from a parent. These genetic changes contribute to the development of a disease but do not directly cause it. Some people with a predisposing genetic variation will never get the disease while others will, even within the same family.

Genetic variations can have large or small influence on the likelihood of developing a particular disease. For example, certain mutations in the *BRCA1* or *BRCA2* genes greatly increase a person's risk of developing breast cancer and ovarian cancer. Variations in other genes, such as *BARD1* and *BRIP1*, also increase breast cancer risk, but the contribution of these genetic changes to a person's overall risk appears to be much smaller. Current research is focused on identifying genetic changes, which have a small effect on disease risk, but are common in the general population. Although each of these variations only slightly increases a person's risk, having changes in several different genes may combine to increase disease risk significantly. Changes in many genes, each with a small effect, may underlie susceptibility to many common diseases, including cancer, obesity, diabetes, heart disease, and mental illness.

In people with a genetic predisposition, the risk of disease can depend on multiple factors in addition to an identified genetic change. These include other genetic factors, sometimes called modifiers, as well as lifestyle and environmental factors. Diseases that are caused by a combination of factors are described as multifactorial. Although a person's genetic makeup cannot be altered, some lifestyle and environmental modifications, such as having more frequent health screenings and maintaining a healthy weight may be able to reduce disease risk in people with a genetic predisposition."

A New Lineage

Adam's rebellion and the introduction of sin and death into the world, caused all humans beings to be genetically pre-disposed and susceptible to the by-products of that sin which includes sickness, disease, and infirmities. As previously stated— Jesus Christ, the last Adam came into the earth free of Adam's genetic pre-disposition and susceptibility, because He was born of a virgin by the overshadowing of the Holy Spirit, Jesus was the first person to be born of the Spirit. Every other human being had to be *born again*, as He told Nicodemus, of the Spirit. Jesus had one birth, when the Word came from Heaven to become flesh, but all other human beings must have two births, to get from earth to heaven.

A female may decide to have a hysterectomy or breast removal, because of a pre-disposition in her family to uterine or breast cancer, but she has no such worry in God's royal family because the Blood gives her *New Genes!* In her earthly family, she may have been abandoned as a child, molested by a family member, or grew up in poverty, but she does not have to feel the stigma of the trauma she experienced by her connection to her first family—She can bury the negative memories associated with the troubles of her biological family, and focus on the amenities and privileges of having the distinction of being a child of God. The Children of God must not be stagnated by memories of past experiences or unresolved issues from their earthly family. Paul's words to the Philippian Church should be heeded— "Brethren, I count not myself to have apprehended: but this one thing I do, forgetting those things which are behind, and reaching forth unto those things which are before, I press toward the mark for the prize of the high calling of God in Christ Jesus" (Philippians 3:13-14). It is extremely difficult to make forward progress while looking in the rear view mirror.

Your first family may be full of alcoholics, drug dealers, ex-convicts, high school drop-outs, perverts, or thieves, but God saved you, so you can be an example to them, and others, of what life can be when a person is adopted into the family of Abba. No longer should you suffer from the effects of your first family, when you have a new lineage and a new name. You may have been denied access and entry to certain places because you did not have the right family connections, or because of your gender or the color of your skin, but being *born again* into the family of God means you not only are part of God's Royal Family, but it also means you have Kingdom Access! There is no greater access.

The *born again* child of God should think, speak and act like "Kingdom Royalty" because that is who they are. The Spirit and the Word instructs the new born how to carry herself. Wealthy people and royalty send their children to prep schools and finishing schools to teach them how to function in society among the elite. The Bible is the instruction book for the Royal Children of God, and His Spirit gives them the wisdom, knowledge and understanding, how "Kingdom children" should live amongst all people. The Spirit of Adoption facilitates the *born again* experience, and gives His Children the honor of being called, Sons of God.

CHAPTER 9

THE SPRIT OF ADOPTION

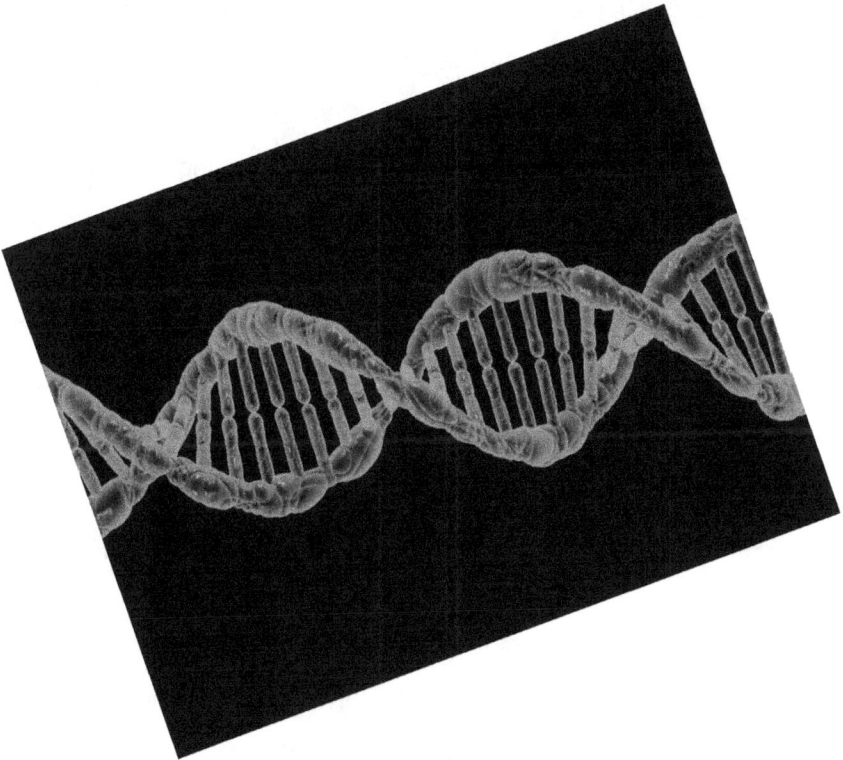

CHAPTER 9
THE SPRIT OF ADOPTION

Baker's Evangelical Dictionary of Biblical Theology, gives this definition of Adoption— "Act of leaving one's natural family and entering into the privileges and responsibilities of another. The Greek word for adoption (huiothesia) means to "place as a son" and is used only by Paul in the New Testament. In the Bible, adoption is one of several family-related terms used to describe the process of salvation and its subsequent benefits. God is a father who graciously adopts believers in Christ into his spiritual family and grants them all the privileges of heirship. Salvation is much more than forgiveness of sins and deliverance from condemnation; it is also a position of great blessing. Believers are children of God"

Paul used the term "the spirit of adoption" in his letter to the church at Rome when he wrote, "For ye have not received the spirit of bondage again to fear; but ye have received the Spirit of adoption, whereby we cry, Abba, Father" (Romans 8:15). A person who is in bondage does not have peace, because they are subject to the whims of the person or thing that holds them captive. A slave is at the mercy of his master, and it does not matter if the master is a person or a thing like drugs, pornography or an addiction to some sexually deviant behavior. Bondage takes away self-determination and autonomy, and that is why people will go to great lengths to be free, including risking their lives. Sin

100

is missing God's mark, and when the mark of God is missed, the ensuing result is the person is taken into slavery by a carnal master. A slave lives in a constant state of worry and fear of what the slave master will do to if he steps out of line. The slave master of all sinners is Satan, the devil. He never commands his slaves to do anything good, because he loves to steal, kill and destroy. When he caused sin consciousness to come into the world, he also caused the souls of human beings to become corrupted. Sin brought soul perversion and spiritual separation from God. Prior to the entrance of sin, Adam had a God consciousness, and he was able to commune with God spiritually, because his spirit was not perverted. Once sin came in, God consciousness was replaced by sin consciousness.

In his book, *The Basics: A Categorical Bible Study,* Gene Cunningham has this quote concerning sin; "What is sin? Lewis Sperry Chafer writes in Systematic Theology that it is essentially a restless unwillingness on the part of the creature to abide in the sphere and limitation in which the all-wise Creator placed him. In general, sin is lack of conformity to the character of God." (Systematic Theology, ed. By John F. Walvoord {2 vols.; Wheaton: Victor Books, 1988}. Cunningham goes on to say, "The only standard for measuring sin is the holy character of God. Sin is sinful because it is unlike God. If we do not have a clear understanding of the character of God, we will never understand sin. The only way to come to an understanding of God is to listen to what He has to say about Himself, to study and meditate on

His Word. How serious is sin? Again, the only way man can understand how awful sin is, is by hearing God's own assessment. Sin is so terrible that the angels who sinned will never escape the Lake of Fire. Sin is so terrible that one act of Adam and Eve brought degeneration and depravity and unfathomable suffering to all humanity. Sin is so terrible that the perfect Son of God suffered to an infinite degree on the cross to redeem all mankind."

With that definition of sin, it is easy to understand why sinners cannot have peace. They must use drugs, alcohol, illicit sex and other vices to escape the reality of the bondage of sin, but eventually they have to come back to the reality that those vices do not give peace. According to the scriptures, the end result of sin is death, but does that mean the sinner will drop dead because of his or her sin? Physical death was one of the results of sin experienced by Adam, Eve and all their descendants, but physical death is not the only type of death that afflicts a sinner. Webster's dictionary defines death as "a permanent cessation of all vital functions: the end of life." Cunningham writes, "Though it is often associated with extinction, death in the Bible never means the end of existence. Instead, it means separation from or the inability to function in a particular realm." He lists the seven deaths that are described in the word.

1. **Spiritual death** is the separation from God. As a result of the fall, all human beings are born spiritually dead,

captives of "the domain of darkness" (Gen. 2:17; Col. 1:13; Rom. 6:23).

2. **Positional death** is separation from sin and the sin nature. Every believer is made spiritually alive and placed in Christ at salvation. We now have the ability to choose every moment whether we will serve our old nature, which will not be taken away until we die physically, or our new nature (Rom. 6:1-4, 10-11; Gal. 2:20; Col. 2:12, 20, 3:3).

3. **Temporal death** is carnality, separation from fellowship with God. Every time we as Christians give in to temptation to sin, we enter temporal death (James 1:15; Rom. 8:2, 6, 13; 1 Tim. 5:6).

4. **Operational death** is separation of our profession of faith from the practice of that faith (James 2:26; Eph. 5:14; 1 John 1:5-6)

5. **Sexual death** is the inability to function sexually (Rom. 4:19-20; Heb. 11:11-12).

6. **Physical death** is the separation of the soul and body, the inability to function in the physical realm (Heb. 9:27; Gen. 5:5).

7. The second death is the judgment of unbelievers, eternal separation from God (Rev. 19-20)

Children of God

"The believer's adoption as a child of God was determined by God from eternity: God "predestined us to be adopted as his sons through Jesus Christ". This adoption is not the result of any merit on the part of the believer, but solely the outworking of God's love and grace (Ephesians 1:5 Ephesians 1:7).

The present reality, of the believer's adoption into the family of God, is release from the slavery of sin and the law and a new position as a free heir of God. Entering into salvation brings the rights and privileges of free sonship: Paul tells the Galatians that Christians were redeemed from the law so that they might receive adoption as sons. As a result, the Holy Spirit comes into the believer's heart crying, "Abba Father" (Gal 4:5). The intimacy of a relationship with God the Father in contrast to the ownership of slavery, is a remarkable feature of salvation." (Baker's Evangelical Dictionary of Biblical Theology - Adoption)

Abba Father

When someone is adopted into the family of God through the born again experience, their spirit is quickened and comes alive spiritually. According to Paul, the Holy Spirit bears witness with our spirit, that we are the children of God. We can only become His children through, "The Spirit of Adoption." When we were aliens and strangers, we were separated from God and considered bastards. Once we become children, through the adoption process, it gives us the opportunity to call God, Abba Father.

God is a Spirit and His children are spiritual beings. Adam and Eve were spiritual beings with a soul and a physical body to house their spirit and soul. When Eve was deceived and Adam sinned, they lost their spirituality and became creatures that operated from a soul-ish nature and not a spiritual one. Sin destroys spirituality and breaks fellowship with God. He does not communicate with our flesh, but with our spirit, so we had to come alive spiritually in order to interact with Him. Once we came alive spiritually, He adopted us; He will not adopt a dead person, because He is not the God of the dead but the God of the living. There is an encounter recorded in Luke 9:60, where Jesus invited a man to follow Him. The man asked Him if he could go and bury his father, then follow Him. Jesus told him, "Let the dead bury their dead: but go thou and preach the kingdom of God. The kingdom of God is all about spreading the good news of spiritual adoption through Jesus Christ.

The Spirit not only paves the way for us to be children of God, but it brings with it certain amenities and privileges. As children of God, Paul says we become, "heirs of God, and join-heirs with Christ." How wonderful the grace of Almighty God is that through Divine enablement and unmerited favor, He seats us in heavenly places with Jesus Christ as heirs of salvation. I concur with the person who asked the question, "Who wouldn't serve a God like this?" I answer that question by saying, a fool, that is who. A loving God who did not leave us as orphans and bastards, but made room for us in His family through the Spirit of Adoption, is the only God I would ever think about serving. It would have been enough for me, if He only rescued me from the wrath to come, but to know that I have a prepared place in heaven with Jesus Christ is humbling and gives me great peace and joy.

Adoption is a wonderful tool that is used to hand pick a child or children to be part of a family. As wonderful as the process is in placing a child in a home, children who are adopted can struggle at times, especially when they find out they are not biologically connected to the family they live with but were brought into the family through adoption. There have also been horror stories of adopted children being beaten, tortured, chained and starved to death. Many adopted children choose to seek out their biological parents, because they have many questions, such as the need to know why they were given up for adoption. Some probably seek out biological parents out of a sense of curiosity, because they want to know where they come from. Through DNA people are able to trace their family tree back many generations.

As a Christian, it is such a blessing to know that Abba Father, picked me to be a part of His family through the Spirit of Adoption. As previously stated, the derogatory term bastard, is used to describe a child or children born to parents who were not married.: In Hebrews 12:8 the Greek word for bastards is *'nothos'*, and it means a spurious or illegitimate son.

Through the Spirit of Adoption, the sinner is delivered from the spirit of bondage to sin and is brought into the family of God, with the rights and privilege of knowing God intimately enough to use the term, "Abba Father." The Holy Spirit facilitates the adoption because according to Second Corinthians 1:22, through Jesus Christ, God established us, anointed us, sealed us and gave us the earnest of the Spirit in our hearts. He told the Ephesians they were sealed with the Holy Spirit of promise when they trusted in Christ after hearing the word of truth and believing it for salvation (Ephesians 1:13). In Ephesians 4:30-32, he wrote, "And grieve not the Holy Spirit of God, whereby ye are sealed unto the day of redemption. Let all bitterness, and wrath, and anger, and clamour, and evil speaking, be put away from you, with all malice: And be ye kind one to another, tenderhearted, forgiving one another, even as God for Christ's sake hath forgiven you." The Spirit of Adoption not only sealed us unto the day of redemption, but it opened the door for us to have new DNA, the Divine Nature of Abba. When we have Abba's Divine Nature, we will not allow bitterness, wrath, anger and malice to control our attitudes and our actions. We will not speak evil, because the heart of flesh is replaced with the mind and heart of the Holy Spirit. Instead of a nature of un-forgiveness, we forgive our brothers and sisters when they transgress against us.

107

Without the Divine Nature of Abba, people would devour one another through un-forgiveness and vengeance. Wrath, anger and malice would be the response to others when they transgress against us. Those attributes of a fleshly stony heart are evident in the people in the world. I am not saying all the people in the world act in such a cold callous manner, what I am saying is, they have the propensity and the proclivity to act that way because of their un-regenerated human nature. Even some religious people exhibit the negatives Paul describes in Ephesians 4:30-32. The Middle East is one of the most religious regions on the face of the earth and it is one of the most violent and one of the bloodiest. Almost daily on the news you see the bitterness, wrath, anger, clamour, evil speaking and malice. Some of the most heinous acts a human being can perpetrate against another are done by some Muslims to other Muslims and some Muslims towards some non-Muslims. I've heard on the news, where a group called Isis had a soldier from the Nation of Jordan in a cave and set him on fire while he was alive. There are many images on the internet of this group beheading people. The carnage they inflict in the name of their god is not contained in the Middle East, but has spilled over into Europe and the United States. They kill men, women and children in the name of their god. If they had the DNA of Abba, His Divine Nature, they would be their brother's keeper and not their brother's killer, like Cain!

As a Christian, it is difficult for me to fathom how people can murder and maim other people in the name of a god, but

108

when I think about it, I realize they are doing it in the name of their religion and the type of god that religion exposes them to. Micah 4:5 declares, "For all people will walk every one in the name of his god, and we will walk in the name of the Lord our God for ever and ever." The name of the Lord our God is Jesus Yeshua, and when we walk in His name we have to walk in love and forgiveness. We have to endeavor to live in peace. Hebrews 12:14 comes to my mind, "Follow peace with all men, and holiness, without which no man shall see the Lord: Looking diligently lest any man fail of the grace of God; lest any root of bitterness springing up trouble you, and thereby many be defiled." It is not easy to follow peace with all men because some men are wicked. As Children of God, Christians are called to a high standard in their living—Christians cannot respond to things like people in the world or people in other religions. We have to respond as our Lord and Savior Jesus would. This does not mean Christians are doormats to be walked on by other people—it means we have to go to great lengths to be at peace, to show the love of Abba Father, to a lost and dying world. The dying world must see the love and light of Jesus shining through us and they must know that the only way to walk in that light and in that love is through the Spirit of Adoption whereby they can cry, Abba Father.

CHAPTER 10
THE SPIRIT OF ADOPTION II

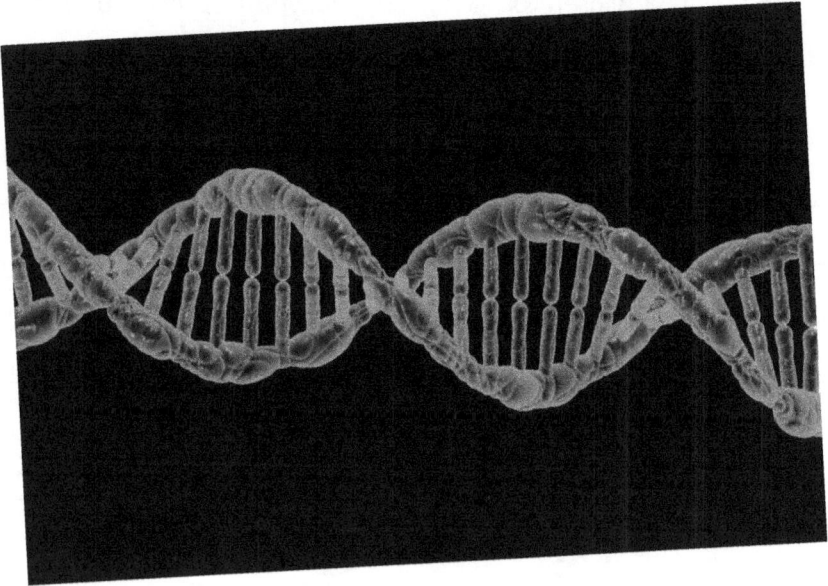

CHAPTER 10
THE SPIRIT OF ADOPTION II

For ye have not received the spirit of bondage again to fear;

But ye have received the Spirit of adoption, whereby we cry,

Abba, Father.

Romans 8:15

I was speaking to my friend and brother in the Lord Dr. Ronald D. Ackerson II and he shared some insight with me on the Spirit of Adoption and it was very profound; so profound that I felt compelled to add it as a chapter, so the reader can be blessed. Dr. Ackerson writes, "It's impossible to discuss the Spirit of Adoption without mentioning the above passage of scripture which remains very familiar even today among saints. This scripture was a discussion Paul had with "all that were at Rome" at that time. All that were at Rome consisted of the early church that was made up of Jew and Gentile. These saints had to come to the initial knowledge and divine revelation of the Spirit of Adoption. Today, the average believer remains unaware of its true biblical meaning and nature; this includes the revelation that the pirit of Adoption speaks of Sonship. As previously mentioned by Fidel Donaldson, the Greek word in this passage of scripture for "adoption" is *"uihothesia"* which means *"placing as a son"* or *"the nature and condition of the true disciples in Christ, who by*

111

receiving the Spirit of God into their souls become sons of God" or
to *"identify those who revere God as their Father, that are pious
worshippers of God, who in character and life resemble God, who
are also governed by the Spirit of God."*

Take notice here that the word adoption has no reference
to what we know it to mean within our western culture. In the
western culture, adoption is defined as a process of taking an
unwanted child of other parents legally as one's own or the
process of the relinquishing of all parental rights to give away an
unwanted child and place them within a system for the purpose of
adoption. This definition is far from the biblical meaning of
adoption which speaks of Sonship; one maturing to adulthood or
coming into a fullness of stature and maturity. With a clear
understanding of this true biblical definition of adoption, the
above mentioned verse takes on a different meaning.
Furthermore, the Amplified Translation reads "For [the Spirit
which] you have now received [is] not a spirit of slavery to put
you once more in bondage to fear, but you have received the
Spirit of adoption [the Spirit producing Sonship] in [the bliss of]
which we cry, Abba Father." Take notice how the Amplified
Translation expounds on the Spirit of Adoption. The Spirit
produces Sonship! In other words, it is the Spirit and this
particular function of the Spirit of Adoption that's responsible for
producing the fullness of one's stature and maturity; ultimately
Sonship!!

With this understanding, every believer is challenged to grow up and mature by having a relationship with the Holy Spirit; the Spirit of Adoption. Many believers measure their maturity in God by the years they have been saved. The number of salvation years has no bearing on Sonship, maturity or fullness of stature. The above mentioned verse further illuminates one's understanding even the more of the fact, that the spirit of slavery works to put believers in bondage AGAIN to the spirit of fear. Notice it said, AGAIN to fear, but we know that fear is a spirit, according to II Timothy 1:7. Please notice the mention of the spirit of fear.

This can be broken down further. The spirit of slavery is an oppressive spirit that keeps one in bondage through fear, control, manipulation, abuse, etc. These spirits work together to create a network of bondage, which can include however many subordinate spirits needed to support the bondage. Keep in mind the root spirit or strongman is the spirit of slavery. This network of spirits causes some believers to live, act, function as slaves or servants, with the mindset to follow; In other words, resulting in many manifesting characteristics of low self-esteem, insecurity, inferiority; all the opposites of the characteristics of Sonship. These spirits steal from many the desire to mature, grow, and come to the fullness of the stature of the measure of Jesus Christ. These feelings produce thoughts of unworthiness; the work of the spirit of slavery. When this happens, it does not matter how much encouragement and support is released to such individuals, the spirits in their lives will always counterattack with a slave or servant mentality. This causes them to reject how God truly sees them and reject the Spirit that's sent to produce and place them as Sons. For many, they would rather remain slaves.

This network of bondage has to be broken. Many are in this arena thinking it is a badge of honor to remain a slave or servant; when they are called to be a Son. This is such an error in the body. John 15:15 reads "Henceforth I call you not servants, for the servant knoweth not what his lord doeth." Jesus is not obligated to reveal anything to a servant or to anyone with a servant mentality. It is important to distinguish between the Sons of God who have a servant's heart and a servant who works in a house. Sonship does not mean we no longer serve, it means we serve from the position of a Son of God and not a hireling. As this is being read, I hope that you see the schemes of the enemy to rob the church as a whole of their maturity, growth, and stature. Please understand, without the Spirit of Adoption, none of these things of our own accord are possible and Sonship is thwarted. We need deliverance in the church to cast these spirits out, up root the spirit of slavery out of the people, and replace those voided areas with the Holy Spirit; the Spirit of Adoption that will produce the necessary Sonship, maturity, growth and fullness of stature in the life of the believer. He predestined us for adoption as sons through Jesus Christ, according to the purpose of his will (Ephesians 1:5).

This scripture speaks of God choosing us before the foundation of the world, for adoption as sons. In other words, for maturity and fullness of stature according to His will. It is the will of God for us to grow and mature. Galatians 4:1 speaks of one being an heir, but as long as he is a child, he differeth nothing from a servant, though he be lord of all!! As long as one remains childish, immature, carnal, he differeth nothing from a servant, meaning that God is not obligated to reveal anything to him who remains a servant, when he has the opportunity to become a son as mentioned earlier. A servant also doesn't have or receive an inheritance. Galatians 4:2 speaks of one in this state as being under tutors and governors until the time appointed of the Father comes forth. That time appointed is a time the Father sees fit, that one has matured to stature of Sonship.

In the Bible, historically, the father at the appointed time would honor the son by calling the elders of Israel and surrounding neighbors to the gate. All would come and the father would place a signet ring on his son in the presence of the Elders of Israel. This was a special occasion that signified that the young man has matured to Sonship and into his inheritance. A relationship with God is based upon one receiving salvation through Jesus Christ. By receiving Jesus, the relationship is established. Even though we were chosen before the foundation of the world, the process to maturity is not something that happens automatically. One that remains immature cannot be trusted with responsibilities reserved for sons. We see this in the life of Jesus when Jesus came to full maturity. The Father gathered everyone to the Jordan River. Before this time, there was very little mentioning of Jesus while He remained immature; going through the process to maturity. At the time appointed by the Father, Jesus comes to the Jordan and receives His public affirmation for all those in attendance to see and behold. The heavens opened up as the Father affirmed His Beloved Son; the Holy Spirit descended like a dove. This was displayed like a signet ring, which represents a seal of authority and power, as He stepped into His Sonship and ultimately His inheritance.

Maturity is an important factor to Sonship. In Luke 15, we see an example of what happens when an immature son receives his inheritance outside of process, and the fathers appointed time. When the younger son asked for his inheritance outside of the process to maturity and the appointed time, notice he being a biological son didn't have any bearing on his development or maturity process; it did not guarantee any special privileges in the process to his maturity; on the contrary, it exposed his immaturity. Sons were expected to be properly placed and receive their inheritance through the maturity process. Thank God we now have the Spirit of Adoption that will help and bring many sons to the fullness of stature, maturity and our inheritance.

The above passage of scripture speaks also of many that are called to Sonship at salvation. Many today, like the young man in Luke 15:11 have their eyes on the inheritance and not on the Father or the process to Sonship. Sonship emphasizes maturity.

Unlike the father in the parable who gave his son his inheritance, God the Father is not going to release our inheritance to us, as long as we remain immature. Remaining immature is to not yield to the teachings of the Holy Spirit which facilitates maturity for Sonship. In other words, you are refusing to grow up and step in your kingdom identity as well as responsibility. Look back at Jesus' identity and responsibilities after His placement to Sonship at the Fathers appointed time at the Jordan River.

After Jesus matured, His appointed time was at the Jordan River for all to witness the Father's affirmation, and the Spirit's confirmation to suddenly be led by the same Spirit in the wilderness. We see Jesus now in the wilderness experiencing attack after attack from the enemy against His Sonship; ultimately, His identity. This was a temptation to Jesus because the enemy was ultimately tempting Him to prove His identity or Sonship with works and not faith alone. This allows us to know that a son that waits for his appointed time from the Father, can stand on faith alone and does not have to prove his identity to the enemy or anybody else works; Jesus did not have to prove His Sonship to the enemy or to Himself with works outside of God's leading and direction. He was mature enough to know who He was and what was entrusted to Him. By faith in His relationship with the Father and the Holy Spirit, He overcame the enemy in every temptation with the Word of God, as the Word of God.

Jesus is our pattern today of true Sonship. I know that many of us have Old Testament characters that we love and like; however, there is no greater example of Sonship and the Spirit producing Sonship than in the life of Jesus. The Apostle Paul wrote the epistles discussing adoption taken from the Roman's way of life. In fact, their legal way of doing things was surely known in those times among all, therefore, no explanation was needed or warranted. They all understood the meaning of the term adoption that was used naturally; even more so when applied spiritually.

The Benefits of Sonship

"Wherefore thou art no more a servant but a son and if a son, then an heir of God through Christ" (Galatians 4:7).

The benefits of Sonship far outweigh the process. The process can be long or short; depending on the Father's appointed time. I believe ones' humility, hunger, thirst and relationship with the Holy Spirit is a major factor in the maturity process. God must trust the son whom he calls forth. The scripture above defines the relationship with the Father as the ultimate benefit of Sonship and not the inheritance. God's Fatherhood far exceeds any amount of wealth & riches one can obtain. Being heirs of God through Christ is a rich revelation all in itself. Once a believer walks out the process to Sonship, under the guidance of the Spirit of Adoption and has come into full stature, there are three benefits of adoption:

118

1. The son is given the Power of Attorney to operate in the Father's name. The son was able to conduct business legally as the father. Jesus walked in this privilege, which means we can also, as joint heirs of Jesus Christ. In John 5:43, Jesus says, "I am come in my Father's name". This was right after His adoption into Sonship. In John 10:25 he states; the works that I do in my Father's name, they bear witness of me."

2. The son received his full inheritance, and has full rights to the father's wealth. Hallelujah!!! The son was able to use the father's wealth, all that was the fathers was his to use. We see Jesus also operating in this benefit of Sonship. He healed the sick, resurrected the dead, and did many awesome wonders. In John 16:15, Jesus declares, "All that belongs to the Father is mine."

3. Sons have the right and privilege to use the Father's Authority, Power, and Ability. This allows the son to function just like the Father on earth; as He functions in Heaven. Jesus also walked in the measure of Sonship, "He stated several times, that He only did what He saw His Father do, and only said what He heard His Father say (John 5:18-19, John 12:49, John 8:28).

With Sonship comes great responsibility. We must walk through the process that God has ordained for maturity, growth, and development. Without a relationship with the Holy Spirit, maturity in the things of God is thwarted, though salvation is established. It is God's will for His Sons to go further in our walk with Him, so that salvation will not become our only experience. He does not want us to forfeit the chance to grow into Sonship. Without Sonship, you will miss out on many of the things God has reserved for you, most importantly you miss out on deep fellowship with HIM, and HIS Fatherhood in your life. Let's Grow up! Let's Mature! Let's be SONS!

CHAPTER 11

SONS OF GOD ARISE

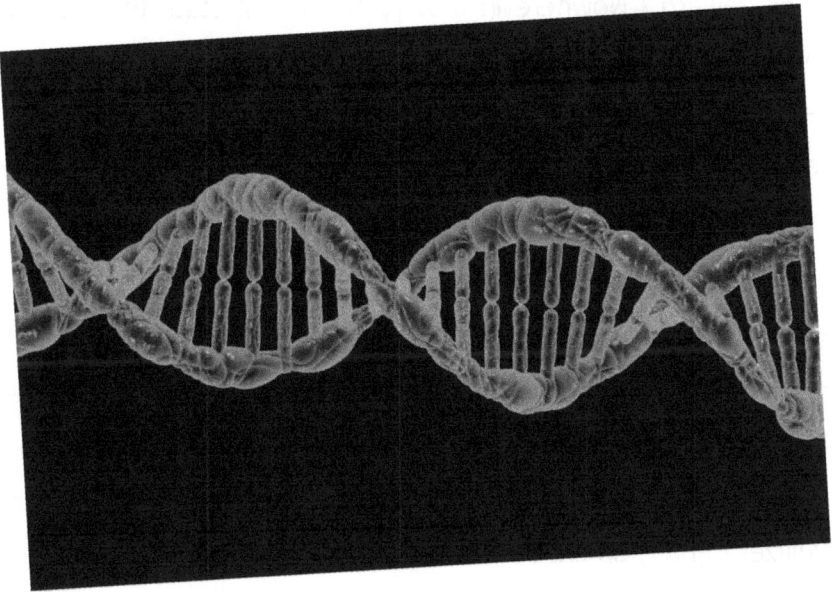

CHAPTER 11
SONS OF GOD ARISE

There are many countries and many societies where sons are preferred over daughters. In some of these societies, when a woman is pregnant with a daughter and not a son, her husband pressures or forces her to have an abortion. In the extreme cases female babies who are killed or abandoned after birth. These practices are widely condemned in the United States and other countries, but ironically, abortion, which is the killing of the unborn baby is legal in the United States. Psalm 127:3 declares, "Lo, children are a heritage of the Lord: and the fruit of the womb is his reward." Nowhere in that verse does it state that sons or male babies are a heritage, but that children, both males and females are a heritage and represent fruitfulness. God looks at female babies as a heritage and the fruit of the wombs as he does with male babies.

I would imagine that the history of the preference of having a son over a daughter in many of these societies is because of a son's ability to go out into the field to work. The son also carries the family name permanently, whereas the daughter adopts her husband's name when she is married. In an online article from Pulitzer Center, on crisis reporting, published September 11, 2013, Carl Gierstorfer wrote, "The New Delhi rape case left the whole world wondering why India is treating its women so badly. In fact, discrimination against women starts in the womb: India has some of the most distorted sex-ratios in the world. There are regions where fewer than 800 girls are born for every 1,000 boys. For many reasons Indian culture prefers sons. An expensive bride-price, or dowry, is only one of them.

So day by day, thousands of parents circumvent rarely enforced laws and have their baby daughters aborted after an ultrasound scan has revealed the sex of the fetus. It is estimated that India has been losing up to 12 million baby girls over the last three decades." With such a horrific decimation of the female population in these countries through the practice of infanticide, there must be a shortage of brides.

Here is an excerpt from an article published in *International Business News*, November 16, 2015 titled: A Deadly Preference For Male Offspring: The Killing Of Baby Girls In India And Pakistan, South Asia's endless and brutal war against its female population took another ghastly turn last week when a Pakistani man admitted to drowning his one-and-a-half-year-old baby daughter (in front of the child's mother) because he had wished for a son instead. Umar Zaib, a 28-year-old rickshaw driver, now under arrest for the murder of his daughter, Zainab, admitted to BBC that he regretted his action, characterizing his horrific act as a "mistake." Zaib was carrying out (to a homicidal extreme) an ancient preference for male offspring in South Asian society and other parts of Asia and the Middle East.

Male and Female Created He Them

When the Bible uses the term "Sons of God," it is not a term used to elevate males over females, or to give credence to the domination and subjugation of women, like you witness in some societies where women have very few rights. Sonship is a term that is not gender specific and speaks more of a spiritual transformation than it does anything physical. The New Testament concept of the Sons of God refers to a remnant of people who have come to a place of maturity in the things of the Spirit of God. In John 1:10-13, the Bible declares concerning Jesus, "He was in the world, and the world was made by him, and the world knew him not. He came unto his own, and his own *received* him not. But as many as *received* him, to them gave he *power* to become the Sons of God, even to them that believe on his name: Which were born, not of blood, nor of the will of the flesh, nor of the will of man, but of God." The "Sons of God" are different from sons or daughters born to earthly parents, because the birth of God's sons is not by human blood or human will but through the Blood of Jesus and the will of God.

The Sons of God have a revelation, a belief and a trust in the Lord Jesus Christ. The Greek word for "received" is, *paralambano*. It means, to receive near, i.e. associate with oneself (in any familiar or intimate act or relation); to assume an office; to learn: It comes from the primary preposition, para which

124

means near; i.e. beside or in close proximity and the word lambano; a prolonged form of a primary verb, which means to take, to get hold of; Through the power of the Holy Spirit. Abba Father draws his children near to Him, so He can shower them with His love and teach them His ways. There is a secret place by God, and in God, that the Sons are being prepared to inhabit. It is a place of intimacy. That is why the remnant church Jesus will return for, is a bride without spot, wrinkle or blemish.

In-order to be called the Sons of God, sons must go through the fire of preparation, to cleanse them of every vestige and residue of the old carnal Adamic Nature. Abba draws them out of sin because of His Divine Power which is far greater than any power, the prince of the power of the air, can exert to keep them bound. The Greek word for power, as John uses it in the text, is the word *exousia*; it means, privilege, force, capacity, freedom, delegated influence: authority, jurisdiction. This is why Paul wrote, "Who shall separate us from the love of Christ? shall tribulation, or distress, or persecution, or famine, or nakedness, or peril, or sword" (Romans 8:35)? Sons of God will not be separated from the love of God because of the trust they have in His name.

When Peter wrote about grace and peace being multiplied to the children of God, he spoke about divine power giving God's children all things that pertain unto life and godliness because of the knowledge of the Father through Jesus Christ. The Sons of

God need not worry themselves about how they will eat, what they will wear or where they will live, because as children of God and citizens of His Kingdom, He adds the things they need as they seek His Kingdom first and all its righteousness. Jesus told His disciples that Gentiles seek after what they shall eat, wear and drink, but our heavenly Father knows the things His children need.

"Behold, what manner of love the Father hath bestowed upon us, that we should be called the sons of God: therefore the world knoweth us not, because it knew him not" (1 John 3:1). If anyone is looking for a reason why God does the things He does for His children, the answer is, He does it because He loves them. When I read 1 John 3:1, I can feel the depth of his question concerning the love the Father bestows upon His children. Imagine the love that an earthly father has for his children, and the sacrifices he is willing to make to protect them and to make sure they succeed in life, then think about the love Abba Father has for His children. In order to understand the depth of the love it took to redeem sinners and prepare them for Sonship, you have to meditate on John 3:16, 2 Corinthians 5:21 and Isaiah 53:10. In my book, *Mercy And The Sufficiency Of Grace,* I asked this question—what parent would be willing to give up their child to die in the place of a murderer, a rapist or a child molester? Not only would a parent not give up a child for someone who is considered a societal outcast, the parent would demand that the person be punished to the fullest extent of the law. God the Father has such great love that He gave up His only begotten Son,

Jesus to be crucified for the sins of the world. Not only did He give Him up to be crucified to redeem a people, He allowed Him to become sin for them, so they could become the righteousness of God. He did not do it grudgingly or with sadness and melancholy—Isaiah said, "Yet it pleased the Lord to bruise him. (Isaiah 53:10). It is quite challenging for me to comprehend this manner of love; a love so deep that it covers a multitude of sin—a love so rich that it caused Abba Father to send heaven's most precious gift to die at the hands of sinners for the redemption and salvation of sinners. It is a love so great that when Jesus hung on the cross in agony, He said to His Father, "Father, forgive them; for they know not what they do" (Luke 23:34). This manner of love did not only provide deliverance from the fiery wrath to come, but it bestows the honor upon the remnant to be called, the Sons of God.

If you are reading this and you feel un-loved, or you feel rejected by the people who should love you because of some transgression you committed—you don't need to spend another moment in torment, because God loves you and has provided the provision for your deliverance. You may feel like your iniquities have separated you from God and your sins have caused His face to be hid from you. You know sin causes a separation and a breach. You may feel like God does not hear you, because you were told God does not hear the prayers of sinners. There is one prayer God always listens to, and it is the prayer of repentance. Take a moment now and repent of any and every iniquity and sin that has caused a separation between you and God. Ask Him to forgive you of the things that caused His face to be hid from you; ask Him to cleanse you by the washing of the Blood of Jesus Christ. You may have committed some wicked acts that have you feeling there is no way God will forgive you, but the sacrifice of Jesus was great enough and strong enough to cleanse you of all sin and unrighteousness. Remember, David sent a man to die so he could cover up the fact that he slept with his wife and impregnated her, but he repented and God forgave him. Read and meditate on Psalm 51, which is David's prayer of repentance to God.

Not Some Cosmic Judge

Don't look at God as some distant cosmic Judge who is ready to punish people for their sins—see Him as He truly is, a loving Father who yearns for men to come to repentance. The story recorded in Luke 15 of the prodigal son is a great example of the loving heart of a father and his willingness to restore the wayward son, who comes to himself, recognizes his sins, and returns home for forgiveness. Although he took his journey to a far country and wasted his substance with riotous living, he never stopped being a son. He only stopped living like a son because he separated himself from his father's presence. Prior to his return home, he planned to tell his father— "And am no more worthy to be called thy son: make me as one of thy hired servants". And he arose, and came to his father. But when he was yet a great way off, his father saw him, and had compassion, and ran, and fell on his neck, and kissed him (Luke 15:19-20). He was not looking to be restored to Sonship, he was willing to be a servant in the father's house, but his father restored him back to his original position by clothing him with the best robe, by putting a ring on his hand, shoes on his feet, and by killing the fatted calf.

Ellicot's Commentary For English Readers has this commentary on the prodigal son's restoration: It is hardly necessary, perhaps, in such a parable to press the symbolic interpretation of each minute detail; but in this instance, the symbolism lies so near the surface, that it is at least well to ask ourselves, what meaning either earlier, or later associations would lead the disciples to attach to them. The "best robe" cannot well be other than the "garment of praise" (Isaiah 61:3), the vesture of righteousness, the new life and immortality with which it is the desire of the penitent to be clothed upon; the ring, as the signet upon the right hand (Jeremiah 22:24), must be the token of the special favour of the Giver, the seal of his "calling and election;" the shoes must answer to that "preparation" or "readiness" which comes from the gospel of peace (Ephesians 6:15), and which makes him eager to do his work as a messenger who proclaims that gospel to others, and which he need not lay aside (comp. Exodus 3:5) even when he treads on the "holy ground" where man holds communion with God, the forgiven and restored son with the Eternal Father.

There is no greater honor anyone can have than to have the title, Son of God bestowed upon them. There is no good deed or act that can earn it because it is bestowed through agape love. No human being should go through life feeling un-wanted and un-loved when the Father waits with open arms to receive them. When a person feels like their life has no value because they are not loved and appreciated, deep depression can cause a suicidal spirit to seize their mind and deceive them into thinking life is not worth living. They may not have received the love of an earthly father or mother; maybe the person to whom they gave their heart and their best years, took their love and kicked them to the curb like a piece of junk; the love of God and the Spirit of Adoption can and will restore that person to a place of peace and joy; A place where they can live a fruitful life and help others to escape the deep, dark place of depression.

Transformation and Renewal

Sonship means everything about the child of God will be transformed and renewed through a mental metamorphosis. The transformation and renewal does not take place with the waving of a wand, but it is a process that begins when the person gets saved. For me, the environment was a prison cell in England, but for others it may be some tragic situation, that led them to cry out to God for mercy. Whatever the circumstance or the situation that led you to call upon the name of Jesus, when you called, He answered and started you on a journey to Sonship. You may be reading this at the present time from a place that is very challenging, a place like a prison, a hospital bed, a half-way house, or a homeless shelter. Believe the Lord, that where you are at the present time, and the condition you are in, is not your final place, but you are in a process of preparation for elevation, as He prepares you for the illustrious title of "Son of God". Please don't allow your current place or state to determine who you are. Please don't allow the opinions of other people who really don't know who you are to impose upon you, their idea of who and what you should be. Please remember what the apostle John wrote in 1 John 3:1, "therefore the world knoweth us not, because it knew him not."

It is amazing that the early disciples did not fully know Jesus' true identity and His mission. This is evidenced by the fact that Philip said to Jesus, "Lord, shew us the Father, and it sufficeth us. Jesus saith unto him, Have I been so long time with you, and yet hast thou not known me, Philip? he that hath seen me hath seen the Father; and how sayest thou then, Shew us the Father" (John 14:8-9? Please don't believe because a person has attended church for a long time, that they know Jesus. The Word and the Father are one, so when the Word became flesh and dwelt among men, it meant the presence of the Father dwelt among them; When Jesus told Philip, "Have I been so long time with you, and yet has thou not known me, Philip?" Philip was looking for the one who was right in front of him but he could not recognize Him. When John the Baptist was in prison, he sent disciples to ask Jesus, "Art thou he that should come, or do we look for another" (Matthew 11:3)? There is no reason to look for another because Jesus has come, and He is the friend that sticketh closer than a brother. If you have been looking for another, then your search is over; just stop looking and receive Jesus! When He came into the coast of Caesarea Philippi with His disciples, He asked them, "whom do men say that I the Son of Man am? When they told Him who the people thought He was, he asked them, "Whom do you say that I am." When they received the revelation of His true identity, He told them flesh and blood hath not revealed it unto them but His Father in heaven.

Don't waste time around vain religious folks who have no clue of the true identity of Jesus and your true identity. The revelation of Jesus Christ comes from Abba Father, through the Holy Spirit. If they had the Spirit of discernment, they would know who you are, because they would be able to look beyond your current state, and see the work He is doing in and through you. Jesus wasn't any less of a Son when He was beaten, battered and left for dead on the cross. It was because He was a Son that He was able to go to the cross and the grave, to gain victory over the wicked one, by getting victory over hell, death and the grave.

You are being prepared for the fullness of Sonship, but your position of Son was sealed the day you were converted. The apostle John went on to write in 1 John 3:2, "Beloved, now are we the sons of God, and it doth not yet appear what we shall be: but we know that, when he shall appear, we shall be like him; for we shall see him as he is." Right where you are at the present time, you must know that you are a Son being prepared for His appearance, so don't allow the severity of your situation to convince you otherwise. You may be reading this and think, if I'm a Son, why am I in this place going through this? Why have the people whom I've helped forsaken me in the time of need? You are going through because you are a Son, chosen to carry your Father's glorious DNA and that is why your purification consist of fiery trials. You're in good company so be of good cheer.

It was Joseph's brothers who threw him into a pit (Genesis 37:24). The people who David helped, picked up stones to stone him when their souls were grieved because the Amalekites burned Ziklag and took their wives and children (1 Samuel 30:6). David said, "Yea, mine own familiar friend, in whom I trusted, which did eat of my bread, hath lifted up his heel against me" (Psalms 41:9). The priest from Jeremiah's own town of Anathoth in Benjamin, sought to kill him because he dared to speak the un-adulterated word of the Lord, prompting God to say this to them, "Therefore thus saith the Lord of the men of Anathoth, that seek thy life, saying, Prophesy not in the name of the Lord, that thou die not by our hand: Therefore thus saith the Lord of hosts, Behold, I will punish them: the young men shall die by the sword; their sons and their daughters shall die by famine: And there shall be no remnant of them: for I will bring evil upon the men of Anathoth, even the year of their visitation" (Jeremiah 11:21-23). Don't be surprised when some of your greatest attacks come from family, so-called friends or even a spouse. You have little or no control over what others do, but you do have control over how you respond. Hold your peace and let God fight the battle. He has chosen you in the furnace of affliction to carry His DNA, and He knows best how to keep you.

Your physical position and situation on earth may be difficult, but know that you have a great spiritual position. Speak and act from your spiritual position in heavenly places, and not from your position and situation in earthly places. In other words, speak position-ally and not situation-ally. Listen to what Paul wrote to the church at Ephesus, "Blessed be the God and Father of our Lord Jesus Christ, who hath blessed us with all spiritual blessings in heavenly places in Christ: According as he hath chosen us in him before the foundation of the world, that we should be holy and without blame before him in love: Having predestinated us unto the adoption of children by Jesus Christ to himself, according to the good pleasure of his will" (Ephesians 1:3-5). Beloved, once again, be of good cheer and rest in the peace of God who handpicked you from the foundation of the world to be a Son. *Sons of God, Arise.* Please do not settle for anything less, when your heavenly Father has chosen you and blessed you with all spiritual blessings in heavenly places in Christ. You cannot afford to give up in the midst of your fiery trials because creation is waiting for your full development, as a Son. A Son endued with power and authority to be used by God to destroy the works of the devil.

134

Chapter 12

THE HEART OF THE FATHER

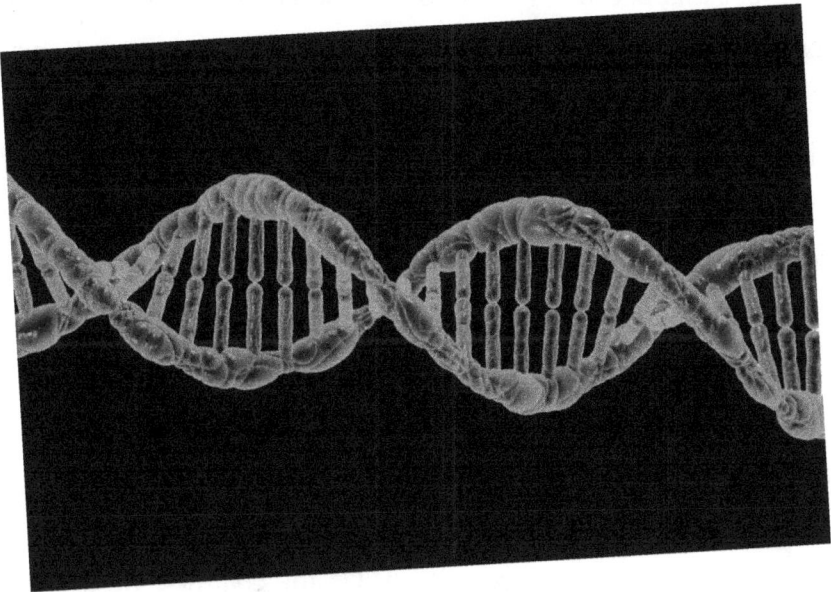

Chapter 12
THE HEART OF THE FATHER

ABBA FATHER

As a heavenly Father, God is perfect in all His ways, which includes the way He deals with His children. Try as they may, many earthly fathers and mothers show favoritism to some children over others. Godly parents do their best to love all their children equally, but good parents are not perfect parents. God is perfect and He loves all His children. I do believe a child of God can feel like a favorite, not because God treats His other children less, but it is because we can only appropriate as much of God's love as we are able to bear, through our yielding ourselves to him. The greater the yielding, the greater the love we will feel from Him. The less we yield is the less of His loving presence we feel.

The idea of God, as a loving Father is a central theme of the Judeo Christian faith. When the disciples asked Jesus to teach them to pray, He instructed them to pray, "Our Father which art in heaven" (Matthew 6:9, Luke 11:2). In the model given to them by Jesus, they were instructed to pray to God as a Father. With Jesus' instructions in mind, Christians must realize we are not part of a religion with a God who is distant, unconcerned and not involved in the lives of His children. On the contrary, we are part of His family.

136

D N A WHO'S YOUR DADDY?

When Jesus was in the Garden of Gethsemane with Peter, James and John, He agonized and told them His soul was exceeding sorrowful unto death; the prospect of becoming sin and being separated from His Father was overwhelming. In that excruciatingly painful moment, Jesus used a term that describes the type of Father He had and all who come to Him for salvation would have. He called God, "Abba, Father" (Mark 14:36). The online site, *gotquestions.org* gives a great definition of the term Abba: "In Scripture there are many different names used to describe God. While all the names of God are important in many ways, the name "Abba Father" is one of the most significant names of God in understanding how He relates to people. The word *Abba* is an Aramaic word that would most closely be translated as "daddy." It was a common term that young children would use to address their fathers. It signifies the close, intimate relationship of a father to his child, as well as the childlike trust that a young child puts in his "daddy." While most people, at least those who do not irrationally deny the existence of God, would claim that all are "children of God," the Bible reveals quite a different truth. We are all part of His creation and under His authority and Lordship and will all be judged by Him, but being a child of God and having the right to call Him "Abba Father" is something that only born-again Christians are able to do, because of the Spirit of Adoption" (John 1:12-13).

A sperm donor can become a father, but as the above referenced article states, God is not only a Father to His children but He is also "Daddy" because of the intimate relationship He has with them; A relationship birthed out of His Agape Love, a love so deep, He will never leave or forsake them. It is the highest form of love an individual can receive. It transcends all other forms of love. When the term, "Father," is used in the Bible to refer to God, it refers to His Divine Nature as a protector and one who loves and adores His children. I don't believe any of the world's faiths or religious beliefs view their god in the way He is viewed in Judeo-Christian thought. Jews and Christians alike hold a biblical view of God as a loving Father or a Daddy who is enamored with His children. Only the children of a household had the privilege of calling their father Abba. Only the children in the household of faith are allowed to call Almighty Yahweh, "Abba, Father."

When I was younger, there was a show on television called, "Wait Til Your Father Gets Home." Whenever the kids would act up, the mother would tell them that in order to get them to behave. The idea being, their father would discipline them for misbehaving when he arrived home. Abba Father does not chasten His children simply because they mess up and He is angry with them. His chastening flows from the love He has for them. Some fathers are sadistic in the manner in which they apply punishment to their children. I've seen stories reported on the news of fathers killing their daughters because they were in a relationship with someone of another faith. I've seen and read other stories of a father killing a child because he rejected the faith of His father and embraced another. Abba Father should be the example of fatherhood for everyone.

The concept of God as a loving Father, is revealed throughout the Bible from Genesis to Revelation. The book of Revelation, the last book of the Bible, records these words spoken by Jesus, "To him that overcometh will I grant to sit with me in my throne, even as I also overcame, and am set down with my Father in his throne" (Revelation 3:21).

When the Lord instructed Abram to leave his country, his kindred and his father's house, He did so because He wanted to prepare him to be the father of many nations. God was going to use him as His vessel to bring a blessing to the families of the earth. After rescuing Lot, the word of the Lord came to him further instructing him that God was his shield and his exceeding great reward. Abram responded by asking God how He would bless him, seeing that he was childless. This was a huge burden and a source of pain for Abram and his wife Sarah. His inability to father a child and her inability to birth out children caused the couple to be stigmatized. Fatherhood was extremely important to the people and culture of Abraham's day.

Although some women in today's society chose not to get married and chose not to have children—many women dream of the day when their hand will be taken in holy matrimony and they are able to start a family. Of course, I am referring to the women who believe in a traditional biblical marriage. Abraham received the word of the Lord concerning his destiny when he was 75 years old and when he was 99 years old, the Lord told him that His covenant was with him and that He had made him a father of many nations. When God spoke those words to him, He changed his name from Abram to Abraham which means a father of many nations. When Abram's name was changed to Abraham, God changed his wife's name from Sarai to Sarah signifying the fact God made her the mother of many nations. Abraham's role as father to many nations is so significant, it is referenced in the story of the rich man and the beggar Lazarus told in Luke 16—when Lazarus the beggar and the rich man died, the beggar was carried to Abraham's bosom but the rich man lifted in hell and was in torment. He was able to see Lazarus in the bosom of Abraham so he cried, "Father Abraham, have mercy on me, and send Lazarus, that he may dip the tip of his finger in water, and cool my tongue; for I am tormented in this flame. The story of Lazarus and the beggar is evidence that hell is a real place, because those words were spoken by Jesus Christ.

In Psalms 27:10 David wrote, "When my father and my mother forsake me, then the Lord will take me up." There are individuals who go through life dealing with rejection, identity crisis and low self-esteem because they were rejected by fathers and mothers. David dealt with that type of rejection and that may have been his motivation for writing those words recorded in Psalm 27:10. *Jamieson, Fausset, and Brown Commentary, Electronic Database by Biblesoft, Inc.* had this to say about

David's words in Psalms 27:10, "David's father and mother forsook him at all events at their death: even in their lifetime, being forced into exile with him (1 Samuel 22:1-3), they were unable to help or shelter him; possibly-such is the selfishness of man in misfortunes-they even blamed him as the cause of his and their trials."

When the Lord sent the prophet Samuel to the house of Jesse, David's father, to anoint the new king—David's father left him out of the identification parade. He paraded seven of his sons before Samuel, but David was left out. There are some sons and daughters reading this right now who were rejected by a father or a mother. David's life is a good example of the fact that you can be forsake by biological parents, but Abba Father will never leave you or forsake you. You may have suffered and still continue to suffer because of rejection from your father, but refuse to be held bound any longer by feelings of inadequacy which stem from someone else's actions. Yes, you should have been treated better and more fairly, but you cannot spend the rest of your life feeling victimized. I implore and encourage you to get rid of the feelings of rejection and low self-esteem because Abba Father desires to make you whole.   He can turn your test into a testimony, your misery into a ministry and your affliction into an anointing. There are some fathers and mothers who hurt their children because they were hurt by their parents.   The saying, "hurt people hurt people" is very profound. The buck has to stop with you; the cycle has to be broken through you. Abba is the type of Father you must model yourself after so you can be the type of father to your child or children that you never had. His Parenting model is the absolute best!

Dysfunction

When the head is not functioning properly the body will be adversely affected; the father is the head of the household and when there is dysfunction in his life, there will be dysfunction in the household. The story of David's encounter with Bathsheba, and the chaos that hit his family, is a great example of the effect a father's behavior can have on his children. When David went with Bathsheba and impregnated her, he called her husband Uriah from the battlefield and encouraged him to go home and spend time with her. His motive for doing that was not pure. He was hoping Uriah would sleep with her and no one would find out, he, David had impregnated her. Instead of going home, Uriah slept at the door at the king's house with all the servants and it was at that point that David decided he had to die. Sometimes the cover up is worse than the original sin. The Lord wasted no time in sending Nathan the prophet to confront him about the terrible sin he had committed. Uriah told him a story about a rich man who had exceeding many flocks but was not satisfied and took the one ewe lamb a poor man had. When the rich man came as a guest at his home, instead of preparing one of the many lambs from his own herd, he took the poor man's one ewe lamb and prepared the meal with it. David's anger was kindled against the rich man and declared that he should surely die and he should restore what he took four-fold because he had no pity. It is amazing how judgmental a person can be when they hear about someone else's transgression.

When David finished speaking, Nathan uttered these famous words to him, "Thou art the man" (2 Samuel 12:7). "Don't throw stones if you live in a glass house" is a very popular saying. When David thought Nathan was speaking about the evil misdeed of another man, he was quick to pronounce judgment; he had no clue that the prophet was referring to him. Once David was exposed, Nathan gave him the word from the Lord as to what the punishment would be. "Now therefore the sword shall never depart from thine house; because thou hast despised me, and hast taken the wife of Uriah the Hittite to be thy wife. Thus saith the Lord, Behold, I will raise up evil against thee out of thine own house, and I will take thy wives before thine eyes, and give them unto thy neighbour, and he shall lie with thy wives in the sight of this sun. For thou didst it secretly: but I will do this thing before all Israel, and before the sun" (2 Samuel 11:10-12). To David's credit, he did not try to justify what he had done, but repented quickly, but the damage had been done and the Lord had spoken. The collateral damage of his actions would play out in his family as his son Amnon raped his sister Tamar and was killed by their brother Absalom. In fulfillment of the word of the Lord, spoken to David by Nathan, Absalom slept with his father's concubines for all Israel to see. Absalom turned the hearts of the people against David, then led a rebellion against him and usurped the throne.

David would not move against Absalom because he loved him. He asked his military leaders to deal gently with him, but Joab, his top military leader ignored him and killed his beloved son, Absalom. I should also mention that David's first child with Bathsheba, which set in motion the horrific chain of events, died in infancy.

Fathers must think about the effect their actions will have on their family. Great destruction came to David's family because of what he did with Bathsheba and his attempt at a cover up. It is better to repent and ask for the mercies of God than to commit a worse sin in an attempted cover up.

The Protector

One of the important roles of a father is a protector for his family. Most if not, all father's would readily put their lives on the line for their children, but there are times when the father's actions open a door of dysfunction in the family. We witness this self-inflicted wound when we examine the life of the first earthly father, Adam. He was placed by God as the protector of the Garden, and was given his wife, Eve to compliment and help him. Abba put them together so they could have dominion, be fruitful, and multiply. They were both created to walk in the love and unity of holy matrimony. When Adam failed in his role as loving protector, the serpent was able to get in the garden and deceive Eve. Women tend to be very nurturing and trusting and that makes them susceptible to be deceived and beguiled by the spirit of the serpent. Many women have opened their hearts to unsuspecting male serpents that walked on two legs, only to find out the individual did not love them, but only came to use them for what they could get.

When John the Baptist came into the wilderness of Judea, preaching the doctrine of repentance for entrance into the Kingdom of Heaven, he was fulfilling the prophetic words spoken by Malachi. John came to prepare the way for Jesus and Jesus came to reconcile sinners back to the Father, so He could release the covenant blessing upon the families of the earth. This is the central message of the Bible—that God the Father loved the world so much that He sent His only begotten Son to die on the cross, so His wayward children could be restored. Were you molested by your biological father, a family member or a friend and has that molestation left you with a feeling of uncleanness. Through His agape love, Abba Father has provided the best cleansing agent and it is the Blood of His Son Jesus. His Blood is able to save from the uttermost to the gutter-most, if you are willing to allow Him into those deep dark places where you have been mentally or emotionally scarred.

The salvation Jesus provides encompasses more than fire insurance or something that allows sinners to escape hell fire and brimstone. It is all about Abba Father, so loving the world that His love would cause Him to rescue sinners who deserved death. Jesus' sacrifice gives the person who is willing to repent access to call God, Abba Father.

Access to Him means unfettered access to His love and all the blessings that is contained in it. Salvation, which is what Jesus' Hebrew name Yeshua means; ensures complete restoration. Salvation provides a complete makeover where the recipient is restored mentally and emotionally. There are television infomercials that feature a before and after picture of a female who had a makeover—After the makeover she looks like a different person. The love of God which facilitated the shedding of the Blood of Jesus gives you a makeover from the inside out—it gives the sinner a new life and a new identity. It translates them from the kingdom of darkness to the kingdom of light where the Father of lights becomes the head of their life.

Someone once told me that a person's view of God as Father is influenced by the type of earthly father they had or did not have. If their earthly father was stern and judgmental, then they view God the same way; if their earthly father was loving and kind, then they view God in that manner. As far as I am concerned, there is only one way to view God and that is the way the Bible describes him. He is loving, He is kind, He is merciful, He is a healer, He is a deliverer etc., His attributes are far too many to list in all the books and in all the computer data bases. However—If I had to use one attribute to represent who God is, and what is His essence, I would use the one found in 1 John 4:8 which says, "for God is love." Everything that we know about God flows from the fact that He is love. All earthly fathers should follow God's pattern of love when dealing with their children and

146

others. Think about it—if the people of the earth truly loved one another as God has loved us, wickedness would not reign in the earth. If Cain loved his brother Abel, the first murder would not have taken place. As a matter of fact, if He loved God, he would not have killed his brother. If Israel loved all his children the way he loved Joseph, there would be no reason for his brothers to hate him, plot to kill him and cast him into a pit.

Earthly fathers can and will come up short sometimes because they are fallible but Abba will never fall short, because He is infallible. James 1:17 describes Him as the, "Father of lights," and further states, "in Him there is neither variableness nor shadow of turning." Since the Bible declares that love covers a multitude of sins, then we all need to spread as much love as we can. Earthly fathers cannot continue to use the excuse of the lack of a loving father in the home when they grew up as a reason for not being more loving; not when the Blood of Jesus Christ has given them access to the throne room of Abba Father. He is a father to the fatherless and will fill every gap.

The greatest access an individual can have is to have access into His presence. Prior to the advent of Jesus' ministry on the earth, sin denied us access to the throne room of God. When God established the Levitical priesthood and selected Moses' brother Aaron as the first High Priest; He was allowed access into the Holy of Holies, but he had to bring the blood of a sacrificed animal for his sins and the sins of the people. Jesus came as the ultimate sacrifice for all mankind and through repentance and the washing of His Blood; we can stand on the words written in Hebrews 4:14-16, "Seeing then that we have a great high priest, that is passed into the heavens, Jesus the Son of God, let us hold fast our profession. For we have not an high priest which cannot be touched with the feeling of our infirmities; but was in all points tempted like as we are, yet without sin. Let us therefore come boldly unto the throne of grace that we may obtain mercy, and find grace to help in time of need." His Blood freed us from the carnal Adamic Nature and gave us access to the Divine Nature of Abba.

Prior to the coming of Jesus, Yeshua, access to Abba Father was granted to the Jews only because of the covenant He made with Abraham. The exclusivity of that access was for a time and a season until God made preparation for Jesus Christ the Savior of the world to come. Through His sacrifice access would be extended to the Gentiles. Jesus told His disciples, "I am the good shepherd, and know my sheep, and am known of mine. As the Father knoweth me, even so know I the Father: and I lay down my life for the sheep" (John 10:14-15). Those sheep were the lost sheep of Israel as Jesus expressed to the Canaanite woman who came to Him for healing for her daughter. He told her, "I am not sent but unto the lost sheep of the house of Israel" (Matthew 15:24). When He was rejected by His own, that rejection opened the door for God's plan to bless the families of the earth through the covenant with Abraham to come to fruition—The Bible states, "He came unto his own, and his own

148

received him not. But as many as received him, to them, he gave power to become the sons of God, even to them that believe on his name: Which were born, not of blood, nor of the will of the flesh, nor of the will of man, but of God" (John 1:11-13).

Remember the words of Apostle Peter, "Grace and peace be multiplied unto you through the knowledge of God, and of Jesus our Lord, according as his divine power hath given unto us all things that pertain unto life and godliness, through the knowledge of him that hath called us to glory and virtue: whereby are given unto us exceeding great and precious promises: that by these ye might be partakers of the divine nature, having escaped the corruption that is in the world through lust" (2 Peter 1:2:4). The carnal Adamic Nature is corrupt and it ruled every one of his descendants, but God's Divine Nature was engrafted into us, when we came to the saving knowledge of His Son, Jesus. Now we trace our spiritual descent from the last Adam, even though biologically, we came from the first Adam. The last Adam, Jesus, is the door through which the sheep enter to find eternal life. I thank God that through Jesus, He has an open door policy, not only for the Jews but for all who come to repentance.

Jesus confirmed the open door and access for the Gentiles with these words, "And other sheep I have, which are not of this fold: them also I must bring, and they shall hear my voice; and there shall be one fold, and one shepherd. Therefore doth my Father love me, because I lay down my life, that I might take it again (John 10:16-17). The Gentiles are the other sheep and thanks be to God for sending Jesus to open the door to the sheepfold not only to save the Gentiles from the wrath to come by giving them access but to give them His DNA.

KEEPER

We recall when God asked Cain where his brother was, he retorted, "am I my brother's keeper?" According to Biblesoft's New

Exhaustive Strong's Numbers and Concordance, the Hebrew word used for "keeper" in Genesis 4:9, is the word *"shamar"*, and it means, to hedge about, to guard; to protect, to attend to. When the DNA or the Divine Nature of Abba is operating in a person's life, he or she will look to be a keeper and not a destroyer. Genesis 4:2 describes Abel as a keeper of the sheep. A different word is used for keeper there and it is the word *"ra 'ah"* and it means, to tend to a flock, to pasture it, to keep company or associate with as a friend. Leaders and lay members in the church should have the Spirit of the Lord, which was the Spirit that was in Abel. The manifestation of the Spirit should be evident in your life as it was evident in the life of Abel. The keeper and protector Spirit should permeate and saturate the attitude and disposition of every child of God. As children of God, we can easily recognize those who do not have the Divine Nature of Abba, but possess the devil's nature for they continually steal, kill and destroy.

Jesus is the ultimate keeper of the sheep. The Bible tells us—He leads the sheep to green pastures and restores their souls when they are overwhelmed. In fact, He made the ultimate provision when He laid down His life for the sheep. He is the supreme keeper and the perfect embodiment of the, Divine Nature of Abba. Satan on the other hand, is the opposite because his nature is not one of keeper or protector, but devourer. Remember Jesus' encounter with some religious leaders who challenged Him when He said God was His Father, He told them, "Ye are of your father the devil, and the lusts of your father ye will do. He was a murderer from the beginning, and abode not in the truth, because there is no truth in him. When he speaketh a lie, he speaketh of his own: for he is a liar, and the father of it" (John 8:44).

Chapter 13

A FATHER AFTER GOD'S HEART

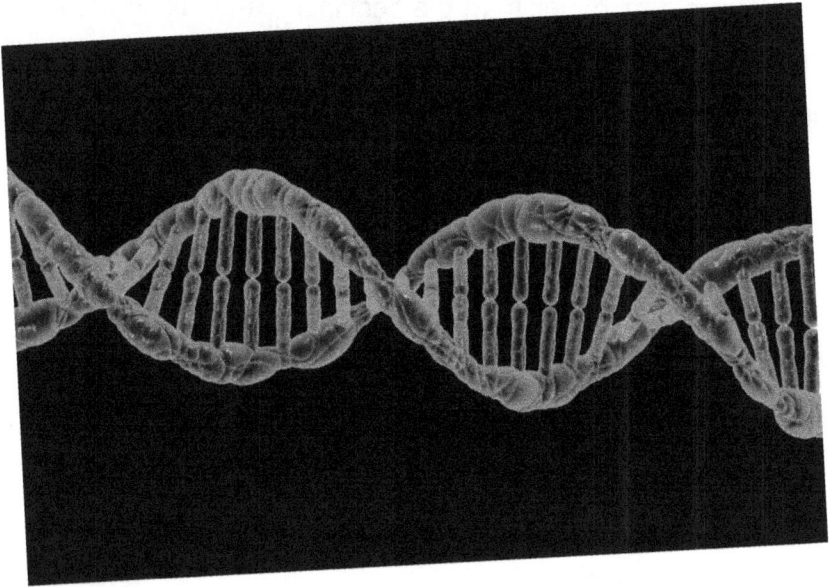

Chapter 13
A FATHER AFTER GOD'S HEART

I was speaking with my good friend, Emmanuel Haniah and inquired if his biological father was active in his life when he was growing up. He told me he does not know who his father is. He spoke very candidly to me about growing up, being one of eight children who had four different fathers. I wanted to know what type of effect growing up without a father had on him, and how it affected the way he approaches fathering his own children. He said he lacked identity and confidence as a young man because he did not feel like he fit in. His other siblings knew their fathers and told him their father was not his. He wondered who he was and felt very uncomfortable when he accompanied his siblings to visit their fathers. While his mom was going through a divorce, she had a boyfriend who she told him was his father. The man denied that he was his father. I can only imagine how devastating that bombshell was for Emmanuel.

His painful experience of growing up without a father made him resolute in his desire to be the best father he could be. Once he was converted and became a Christian, he was able to learn what a good father was, from studying the Bible and learning the attributes of Abba. Those attributes were on display in the lives of strong Christian men in the church he attended. Once he was married and started having children, he committed himself to making sure he was a father who showered them with love. He

153

purposed in his heart to keep his family together, because he knew firsthand the effect growing up without a father has on children. Unfortunately, his wife left him for another man and left him as the primary caretaker of seven children. He had to grieve for himself and grieve for his children, but he was determined to use the abandonment as a stepping stone and not a stumbling block. He told me that he sees the confidence in his children that he never had growing up, although their mother is not in the house. He attributes their confidence to the grace of God, and his dedication to providing a home for them with a Biblical foundation and a lot of love. God bless you Emmanuel, you are one of the most dedicated fathers I have ever met!

Triumph Over Tragedy: R.I.P Michai!

My family experienced a tragedy of immense proportions and that tragedy brought out the protector in me. On December 16th I woke up and gave the Lord thanks for blessing me to see the dawning of a brand new morning. I have a brother and a sister who celebrate birthdays on the 16th of December and I planned on calling them to wish them a happy birthday. It is amazing how quick things can change. Half way through the day, my daughter Makeda called her mom to say Michai, our newly born grandson, was not doing well. We thought it was just another episode that would pass; after all, he had survived being born three days shy of six months, survived the heart murmur that caused him to have an operation, and had overcome many

154

other issues he encountered as a child born prematurely. Makeda called back again, and my wife could hear the distress in her voice, so we dressed quickly and headed to the hospital. When we arrived, the doctor informed us of the gravity of the situation. I was in complete shock, when the doctor said he probably would not make it. He had contracted some bacterial infection and was also dealing with a condition known as NEC, which is a form of infection in the bowels. We stayed at the hospital for hours as the medical staff worked to save his life. We were actually in the room when his tiny heart stopped, and they worked diligently to resuscitate him. We breathed a sigh of relief when his heart began to beat again, and they were able to stabilize him, although he remained in critical condition. The doctor told my daughter to get some rest, and my wife and I headed home, exhausted and drained physically and emotionally. We continued to pray for the will of the Lord to be done because we did not want him to suffer. It was difficult to process that just a few days before, my wife and I were at my daughter's baby shower and were eagerly counting the days as we anticipated our grandson, coming home

At around four twenty-five in the morning, my wife jumped up and said, "The baby is gone." I will never forget those words as long as I live. When she jumped up, I was shocked out of sleep and awoke feeling like I had been plowing a field all night long. While we were on our way back to the hospital, we got a call that his heart started again, so hope and optimism returned. To say we were on a rapidly moving roller coaster would be an understatement. When we arrived at the hospital, our hopes were dashed again, as he had taken another turn for the worse. The medical staff were trying to find a suitable vein to give him an intravenous PICC Line, in order to get more antibiotics into his system. They were never able to find one. When I stepped into the room, I was overcome with emotions as I saw his tiny body hooked up to a breathing apparatus that shook his little frame as it pumped air into his lungs. The nurse was giving him blood, and as I looked at his tiny frame, I couldn't help thinking that I would trade places with him instantly if I could. His stomach was not moving, so I knew he was totally dependent on the breathing machine.

My heart bled, as I saw my daughter turn her face to the wall and sobbed uncontrollably. I wanted to save her. I wanted to make the unfolding tragedy go away as if it was just a terrible nightmare. I wanted to protect her from the pain she was feeling. I wanted to abate the reality of what could possibly happen. I knew she felt helpless as she watched the doctors and nurses attempt to save her only child, who never had the opportunity to come home. From the time he was born on September 30th, she had visited him in the hospital every day. Our freezers were full of bottles of breast milk that she pumped. Her apartment was full of the many gifts she received at the baby shower. I stepped outside of the room and stood watching, because I did not want to be in the way of the medical professionals. I prayed profusely for my grandson, but after a while, the doctor came out and uttered the words, "I'm sorry." Michai was gone, but he would never be forgotten. The moment was terribly bitter-sweet. On the one hand, he was not suffering anymore, but on the other hand, I wondered why he had to go through all that he had gone through, only to lose his life at the end. We were directed to a waiting room where the doctor came and spoke to us followed by a nurse. Michai was cleaned up and brought into the room. My wife held him, as I buried my face in my hands sobbing. I was overwhelmed by the immensity of the situation.

I can only imagine the depth of the pain and sorrow a parent feels when he or she loses a child. I knew I had to be there for my daughter as a father and a daddy. My mind went back to the years when I ran the streets and was not there for her and her siblings, but now I was determined to be strong for her. I felt the pain Makeda, Archie, Michai's dad, and my wife were carrying. I had to find a way to compose myself, so I could be strong for them, because that is what a father or protector does. As a grandfather, I felt the pain of the loss as if it was my own son. I knew my wife was feeling deep sorrow because Makeda is her only daughter out of eight children, and to watch her deal with such a major tragedy had to be extremely difficult. I believe the loss of a child affects a mother in a greater way than it affects anyone else. I know fathers feel the sting of the death of a child, and that cannot and should not be diminished, but a mom carries the child in her womb from the time of conception and is the first person to embrace the child when he or she enters the world. The mother- child relationship is a very special one, and most mothers carry the feelings of the loss of a child for the duration of their lives.

Though I wasn't able to stop the tragedy from occurring, though I wasn't able to spare her the pain of losing her precious seed, though I couldn't protect her from the inevitable fate of Michai, I was able to undergird her with strength and the peace of just having daddy there. My presence was invaluable. God couldn't physically hold her, but I was able to wrap my arms around her, to hold her securely in my arms, and impart grace and comfort in the time of trouble. I was able to reassure her of God's sovereignty and unfailing love. I was able to point her towards His desire and ability to comfort, help and sustain her in her time of despondency. I knew God would eventually give her beauty for ashes, but at that moment I needed to make sure a root of bitterness did not take root in her heart.

Call Me Mara

How ironic it is that we gave Makeda the middle name Naomi. The name Naomi means, "*The loveable, my delight.*" We had no inclination that when we named her after the Biblical character— she would suffer the same loss as her namesake. After Naomi lost her husband and two sons, she told the people of her town, "Call me not Naomi, call me Mara: for the Almighty hath dealt very bitterly with me. I went out full, and the Lord hath brought me home again empty: why then call ye me Naomi, seeing the Lord

158

hath testified against me, and the Almighty hath afflicted me? (Ruth 1:19-21). Mara means, *bitter; sad.* Little did Naomi know that God would turn her tragedy into triumph, as her daughter in-law Ruth married Boaz, The Kinsman Redeemer, and out of that union a lineage was started, that birthed the great king David and the greatest King of them all, King Jesus!

I know my daughter Makeda Naomi Donaldson is finding it extremely difficult to feel loveable or delightful in the midst of her loss, but I believe, by faith, that out of the death of her precious son, Michai, God is going to bring forth fruitfulness.

Chapter 14

IMAGE OF MY DADDY?

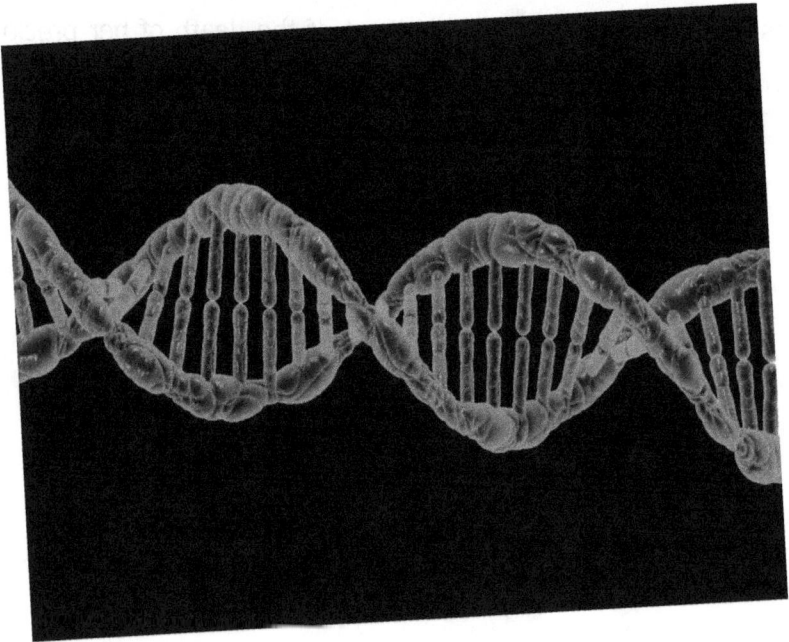

Chapter 14
IMAGE OF MY DADDY?

In the manner in which natural DNA dictates everything about you, such as eye color, bone structure and blood type—the Born Again believer's spiritual DNA, which is transferred to us, from God, through the Blood of our Lord and Savior Jesus Christ— should be the bench-mark of our Divine spiritual identification. Spiritual DNA from God should bring transformation to your life which is seen and manifested as your character traits become more Christ-like and less fleshly.   When you look at a person in the natural, you can see the resemblance they have to their family members. They will look, sound and even act like their relatives.

Children resemble their parents because they get their natural DNA from both of them. Has someone ever told you, "you look just like your daddy" or "you look just like your mom"? As a child of God that is exactly what is supposed to happen to you. When you are in the company of someone who knows your Spiritual Daddy, they are supposed to say, "you not only look just like Him but you act just like Him".   Half of your genome is derived from your mother's egg and the other half from your father's sperm. In the new birth or what I call the re-birth, we get all our spiritual attributes and characteristics from Abba Father. These attributes and characteristics should define who we are— They should show the world what the Divine Nature looks like. People can't see God but they should be able to see Him in us.

161

Spiritual DNA changes our characteristics and qualities and helps us to counteract the negative traits and biological tendencies inherited through our natural DNA. We can determine how an earthly relative looks and acts, based on seeing them in person, but since God is a Spirit—we see Him through His Word and through His children who carry His DNA.

The Word

In the article, Explore DNA: An Overview of DNA Functions", the writer states, "DNA holds the code for proteins, which are complex molecules that do huge amounts of work around our body. Information in DNA is initially 'read' and then it is transcribed into a messenger molecule. After, the information held in this messenger molecule is translated into a 'language' that the body can understand. This language is one of amino acids, which are also known as the building blocks of proteins. It is this specific language that dictates how the amino acids should produce a particular protein." As a child of God, you must read and meditate on His word if you are to be prosperous and have great success. When the child of God is fed a steady diet of His word, the Holy Spirit illuminates the word so it nourishes their spirit, soul and body. Joshua 1:8 gives us these instructions, "This book of the law shall not depart out of thy mouth; but thou shalt meditate therein day and night, that thou mayest observe to do according to all that is written therein: for then thou shalt make thy way prosperous, and then thou shalt have good success."

Natural DNA has a code of instructions for the function of the body and the Word of God gives the code or the instructions how the child of God's body should function. This function can only take place when the body is being directed by a renewed mind which comes through a renewed nature.

The LOGOS Word, is the DNA of every *Born Again, Spirit Filled Christian* because it is our blueprint for life. It has the genetic instructions that teaches us how to be Christ-like, while the Holy Spirit gives us the strength and the discipline to resist the constant encroachment of the carnal nature. The psalmist David declared, "thy word have I hid in mine heart, that I may not sin against thee" (Psalm 119:11). The heart represents the soil and God's Word is the seed that is planted there so His children can live fruitful lives. The unadulterated word of God is the milk and the meat needed by His children to develop into mature Christians. There was a time in Jesus' life where many of the disciples turned back from following Him because He said, "no man can come unto me, except it were given unto me by my Father." At that point, He asked the twelve if they would go too, and Peter answered Him, "Lord, to whom shall we go? Thou hast the words of eternal life" (John 6:65-68). The prophet Jeremiah declared, "Thy words were found, and I did eat them; and thy word was unto me the joy and rejoicing of mine heart: for I am called by thy name, O Lord God of hosts" (Jeremiah 15:16). In the same manner the Word of God holds the instructions for His children's growth and development. Psalm 107:20 declares, "He sent his word, and healed them, and delivered them from their destructions." The Centurion told Jesus, "Lord, I am not worthy that thou shouldest come under my roof: but speak the word only, and my servant shall be healed" (Matthew 8:8).

When our spiritual caloric intake consists of a steady diet of the Word of God, our attitudes will reflect God's Divinity and not Adam's carnality.

Chapter 15

GLORY CARRIERS

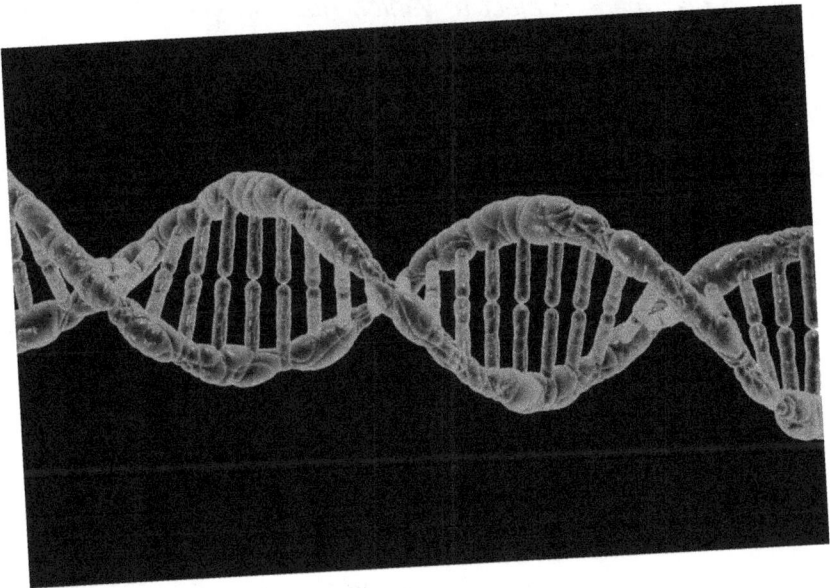

Chapter 15
GLORY CARRIERS

"The Spirit itself beareth witness with our spirit, that we are the children of God: And if children, then heirs; heirs of God, and joint-heirs with Christ; if so be that we suffer with him, that we may be also glorified together. For I reckon that the sufferings of this present time are not worthy to be compared with the glory which shall be revealed in us. For the earnest expectation of the creature waiteth for the manifestation of the sons of God. For the creature was made subject to vanity, not willingly, but by reason of him who hath subjected the same in hope, Because the creature itself also shall be delivered from the bondage of corruption into the glorious liberty of the children of God. For we know that the whole creation groaneth and travaileth in pain together until now. And not only they, but ourselves also, which have the firstfruits of the Spirit, even we ourselves groan within ourselves, waiting for the adoption, to wit, the redemption of our body" (Romans 8:16-23).

The Process

I had to start this chapter with these scriptures because they encapsulate so much of what this book is all about. It's the process we must endure to carry the glorious DNA of God, our Abba Father, and to have the distinction of being called "Sons of

166

God." This distinction will only be bestowed on those who are willing to endure present suffering.

The glory, the manifested Sons will walk in, puts all present suffering in perspective. Meditate on the glory which shall be revealed once we graduate from the class of fiery trials. Every promotion to another dimension of glory requires Sons to endure present suffering, which is part of the preparation process to be glory carriers. When you manifest as a Son of God, you will have His likeness, image and countenance which Adam and Eve had before the fall. You will be able to endure hardship like a good soldier of the Lord. You will be like the three Hebrew boys who refused to bow to the king's idols, but chose to stand for God in the midst of the fiery furnace, and had the honor and the privilege of having "the fourth man in the fire" who had the form of the Son of God with them. Like atoms of Carbon that must endure intense heat and pressure to become a Diamond Rock—Sons of God must endure to have Christ, the Solid Rock formed in them.

You are called to run a race as a Son, and it has to be run with patience because it is an endurance race. Sons have been set apart or consecrated by the baptism of Holy Ghost Fire, which facilities the sanctification process—That process leads to future glorification. The glory will not be carried by any and everybody; only the remnant who are willing to endure the process of purification by fire. It is a purging and purifying fire that burns away the dross that causes you to be lackluster. This remnant will radiate the glorious praises of God like a flawless diamond radiates light. That praise must be pure and it must come through vessels who have been fire baptized. The present suffering may be rough like an uncut or unpolished diamond, but continue to endure because there is Divine purpose to your pain. You are in training for reigning, and present suffering is an integral part of that training.

God's Praises

The separation and preparation of the Sons of God have a multifaceted purpose. The ultimate goal is for God to have a remnant of glory carriers who will show forth His praises throughout the ages to come. These Sons will alleviate creation from its groaning. The Apostle Peter confirmed this when he wrote in 1 Peter 2:9, "But ye are a chosen generation, a royal priesthood, an holy nation, a peculiar people; that ye should shew forth the praises of him who hath called you out of darkness into his marvelous light." The sons of God are chosen for purification by fire in order to be tabernacles or vessels. They are called out of dark places and situations to manifest the Father's praises. Some of us came from some very dark places, and some very dark deeds, but the darkness could not hold us. Our sinful deeds and ways were broken because we were chosen to walk in His marvelous light.

When Peter used the word, "praises," it is the Greek word, *arête* and it means more than clapping your hands, patting your feet or singing a song; it means, manliness, valor, excellence and virtue. It comes from the root word, *arrhen* or *arsen*; which means, male (as stronger for lifting) and from the word, *airo;* a primary root which means: to take up or away; to raise (the voice), the mind, specially, to expiate sin: For the purpose of comparison, let's look at the Old Testament Hebrew word, *nasa'* (Psalms 4:6) (naw-saw'); it means; to lift, accept, advance, arise, to bear up or to bring forth; to burn or to carry away. The Sons of God in the ages to come will radiate the glory, the majesty, and brilliance of His light. Their countenance will show His strength, His valor, His excellence and His virtue; it will show that He has lifted them out of darkness into the marvelous light of His glory. The Hebrew word, *nasa* brought to my mind the name of the United States government agency responsible for the civilian space program as well as aeronautics and aerospace research. NASA has rockets that take men and women to outer space, but it is the Divine Power of God which lifts men and women out of darkness into His marvelous light. He mounts us up with wings of eagles so we can run and not be weary, walk and not faint (Isaiah 40:31).

Overcomers

By the power of Abba Father, we are able to overcome every negative situation that represents the weight of gravity which seeks to keep us grounded. Gravity is defined as: The force that attracts a body toward the center of the earth, or toward any other physical body having mass: extreme or alarming importance; seriousness. *Dictionary.com* defines it this way: the

169

force of attraction by which terrestrial bodies tend to fall toward the center of the earth: heaviness or weight: serious or critical nature. The book of Hebrews instructs us to put aside every weight and the sin that doth so easily beset us and run with patience the race that is set before us. (Hebrews 12:1). Remember, one of the root words for praises is the word *airo*, which means: to lift up; to take up or away; figuratively, to raise (the voice), the mind. God's Divine Power is preparing His Sons for liftoff; like Eagles they are preparing to soar. In an article in *Space.com* titled, Weightlessness and its Effect on Astronauts, contributor, Elizabeth Howell wrote, "The sensation of weightlessness, or zero gravity, happens when the effects of gravity are not felt. Technically speaking, gravity does exist everywhere in the universe because it is defined as the force that attracts two bodies to each other. But astronauts in space usually do not feel its effects. God may not pull you out of the grave situation, but He will keep your mind in perfect peace, so you will not feel the negative effects of it.

The International Space Station, for example, is in perpetual free-fall above the Earth. Its forward motion, however, just about equals the speed of Its "fall" toward the planet. This means that the astronauts inside are not pulled in any particular direction, so they float. God's power is like a rocket booster that gives us the thrust to rise to heavenly places, because the only weight we are to carry, is the weight of His glory. According to *Wikipedia, The Free Encyclopedia*: Solid rocket boosters (SRB), or solid rocket motors (SRM), are used to provide thrust in spacecraft launches from the launch pad up to burnout of the SRBs. The NASA Space Shuttle used two Space Shuttle SRBs, which were the largest of their type in production service. The propellant for each solid rocket motor on the Space Shuttle weighed approximately 500,000 kg. The Holy Ghost is the child of God's propellant because He gives us the ability to walk in the *dunamis* miracle power and the *exousia,* the delegated jurisdiction and influence of Abba Father. Compared to liquid-fuel rockets, the solid-fuel SRBs are advantageous for the purpose of boosting launches, because they provide greater thrust and do not have the refrigeration and insulation requirements of liquid-fueled rockets. Greater thrust means the Children of God are able to rise above any and every situation, because the Holy Spirit gives them the boost and the thrust needed for lift off and maintenance of high altitude.

Groaning and Travailing

The apostle Paul told the church at Rome, "For we know that the whole creation groaneth and travaileth in pain together until now" (Romans 8:22). The Greek word for groaneth is—*sustenazo*; it means: to moan jointly, experience a common calamity: groan together. The common calamity is the sin of rebellion from whence all other sins emanate. It affected all of creation, which caused corporate suffering. The Bible is replete with examples of the effects of sin in the lives of people and its effect on His creation. "And unto Adam he said, Because thou hast hearkened unto the voice of thy wife, and hast eaten of the tree, of which I commanded thee, saying, Thou shalt not eat of it: cursed is the ground for thy sake; in sorrow shalt thou eat of it all the days of thy life; Thorns also and thistles shall it bring forth to thee; and thou shalt eat the herb of the field; In the sweat of thy face shalt thou eat bread, till thou return unto the ground; for out of it wast thou taken: for dust thou art, and unto dust shalt thou return"(Genesis 3:17-19). The evidence of the generational curse that came through Adam is found in Genesis 4:10-12, when God said to Adam's son, Cain, "What hast thou done? the voice of thy brother's blood crieth unto me from the ground. And now art thou cursed from the earth, which hath opened her mouth to receive thy brother's blood from thy hand; When thou tillest the ground, it shall not henceforth yield unto thee her strength; a fugitive and a vagabond shalt thou be in the earth."

Sinners who refuse to turn from their wicked ways and accept Jesus as their Lord and Savior, are fugitives and vagabonds who make a futile attempt to flee from God's divine gaze. On page 43 of his book, The Character of God: Discovering The God Who Is—R.C. Sproul wrote, "For those who have tasted the sweetness of the forgiveness of and reconciliation with God, His ubiquity is good news. But for those who remain hostile and estranged from God, His omnipresence is very bad news. There is nothing a fugitive would want to hear less than that his pursuer is everywhere. There is no place to hide from an infinite spirit. His eye is on the sparrow when it falls. His eye is also on the thief when he steals. There are those who hate God's presence because they cannot stand His gaze. But for those who love His appearing, the presence of God is like soothing music." Adam and Eve made a fruitless attempt to hide themselves from the gaze of God and their son Cain feigned ignorance as to the whereabouts of his brother, Abel. Sinners have been making futile, fruitless attempts to cover up their sins ever since. It's amazing the lengths people will go to in order to hide their transgressions from others, not realizing that they may hide from people, but it is impossible to hide from God.

Our hiding places will be uncovered by God eventually, so it is best to confess and repent so fellowship with Him can be restored instead of living in fear of being caught. Men do not have to live separated from God anymore. Jesus came and provided redemption and reconciliation for those willing to accept Him. You can have the assurance of Sonship, right standing, and complete forgiveness through His Blood. You can become a new creature, forsake the works of darkness and dwell in God's Glorious light. You, too, can be a glory carrier who will show forth His praises. When you have His DNA: There will be no ambiguity concerning: Who's Your Daddy!

FIDEL M. DONALDSON

D N A WHO'S YOUR DADDY?

Bibliography

American Society of Hematology (Online version)

Baker's Evangelical Dictionary of Biblical Theology (Online version)

Sproul, R.C. The Character of God: Discovering The God Who Is. Ann Arbor, Michigan: Vine Books: Servant Publications, 1987

Biblesoft's New Exhaustive Strong's Numbers and Concordance with Expanded Greek-Hebrew Dictionary. Copyright © 1994, 2003, 2006 Biblesoft, Inc. and International Bible Translators, Inc.)

National Science Foundation (Online version

Scitable by nature education

Smithsonian.com

5 cool things DNA testing can do

By Jacque Wilson, CNN

http://www.cnn.com/

175

FIDEL M. DONALDSON

www.ingramcontent.com/pod-product-compliance
Lightning Source LLC
Chambersburg PA
CBHW070757100426
42742CB00012B/2172